WORLD'S BEST GUITAR LEARNING SYSTEM

ChordBuddy SONGBOOK
VOLUME 2

ISBN 978-1-4950-2271-5

7777 W. BLUEMOUND RD. P.O. BOX 13819 MILWAUKEE, WI 53213

For all works contained herein:
Unauthorized copying, arranging, adapting, recording, Internet posting, public performance,
or other distribution of the printed music in this publication is an infringement of copyright.
Infringers are liable under the law.

Visit Hal Leonard Online at
www.halleonard.com

www.chordbuddy.com

4	Ain't That a Shame	17	Cindy
5	All Night, All Day	28	Closer to Free
6	Aloha Oe	30	Cockles and Mussels (Molly Malone)
8	Amanda	32	Down at the Cross (Glory to His Name)
10	Authority Song	34	Early Mornin' Rain
7	Barbara Ann	36	Every Rose Has Its Thorn
12	Beautiful Brown Eyes	38	409
14	Blue Eyes Crying in the Rain	40	Girls Just Want to Have Fun
13	Blue Moon of Kentucky	42	Good Riddance (Time of Your Life)
16	The Blue Tail Fly (Jimmy Crack Corn)	44	Great Balls of Fire
18	Boot Scootin' Boogie	46	The Green Door
20	Brand New Man	33	Have You Ever Seen the Rain?
22	Call Me the Breeze	48	Hush-a-bye
24	Chantilly Lace	50	I Surrender All
26	Cherry, Cherry	51	I've Got Peace Like a River

52	It's Hard to Be Humble	78	See You Later, Alligator
54	Leaning on the Everlasting Arms	80	Stand by Me
56	Learning to Fly	82	The Streets of Laredo
58	Lookin' Out My Back Door	84	Stuck on You
55	Nearer, My God, to Thee	86	Sugar, Sugar
60	The Old Rugged Cross	88	Surfin' U.S.A.
61	On the Turning Away	90	Sweet Home Chicago
62	One Love	92	Too Much
64	Party Doll	83	Turkey in the Straw
66	Rock Around the Clock	94	Up Around the Bend
68	Rock Me	96	When You Say Nothing at All
70	Rockin' Robin	95	Willie and the Hand Jive
72	Sad Songs (Say So Much)	98	Yakety Yak
74	Save Tonight	100	The Yellow Rose of Texas
76	The Scientist	102	You'll Accomp'ny Me
		104	Strum and Pick Patterns

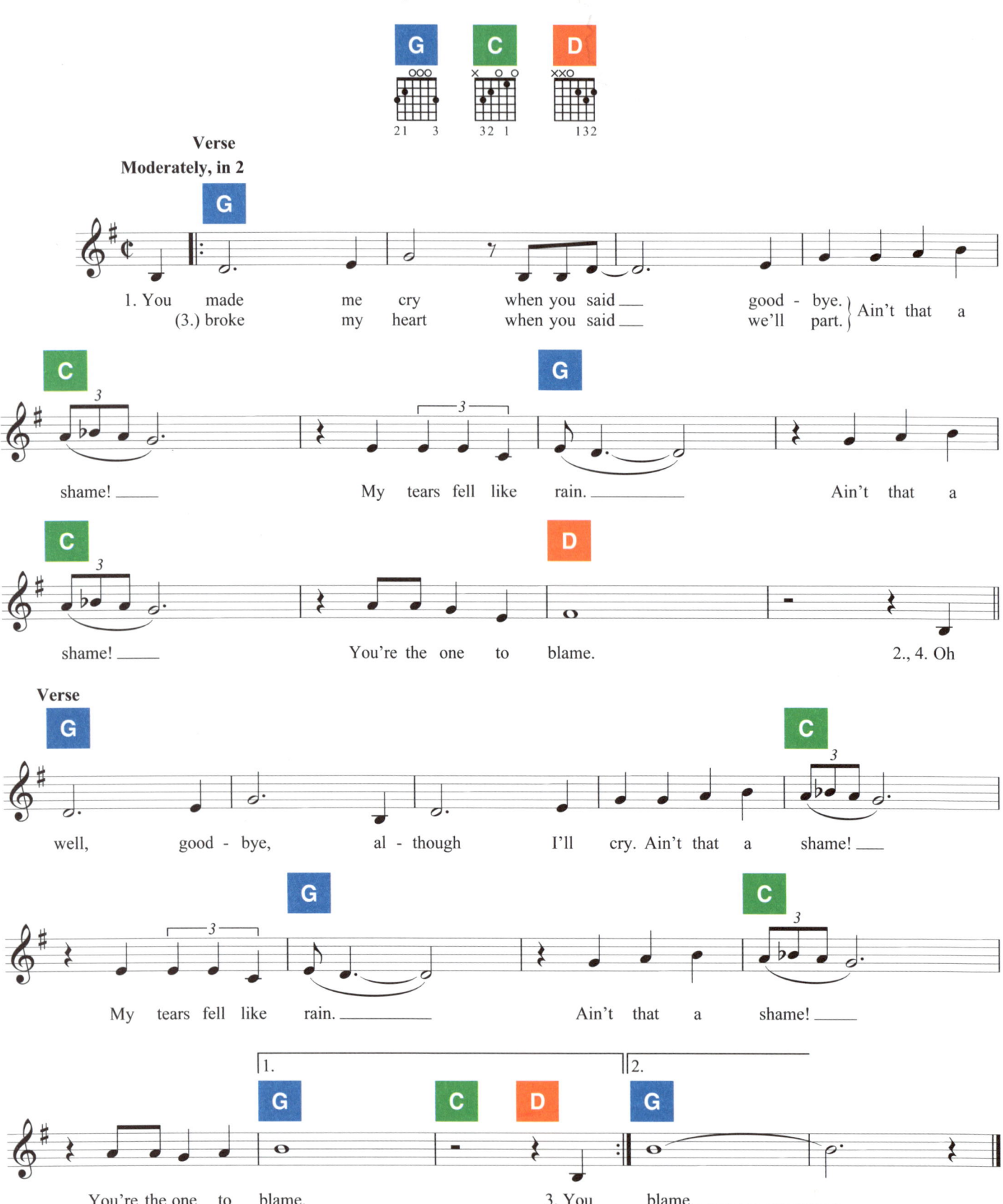

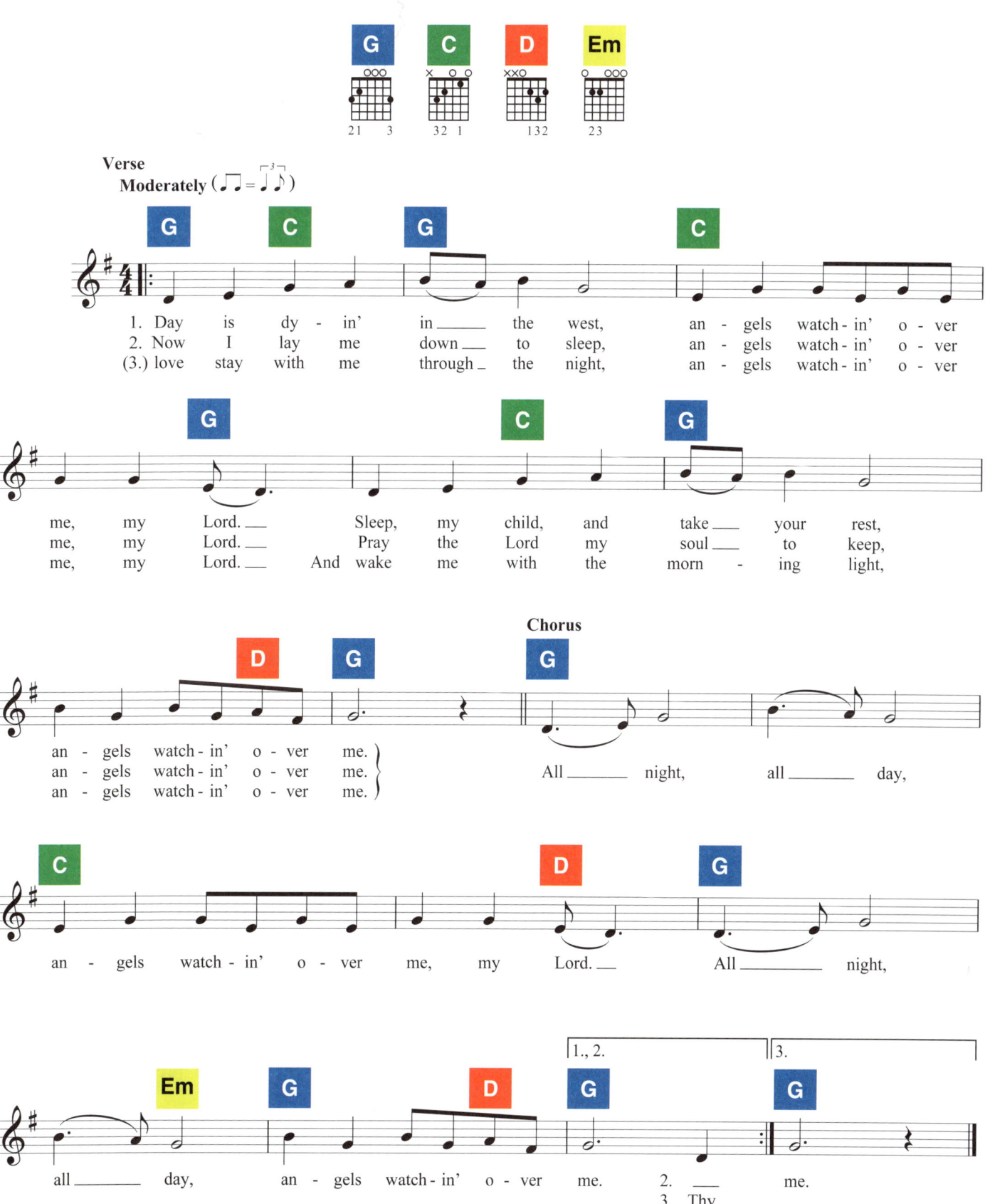

Aloha Oe

Words and Music by Queen Liliuokalani

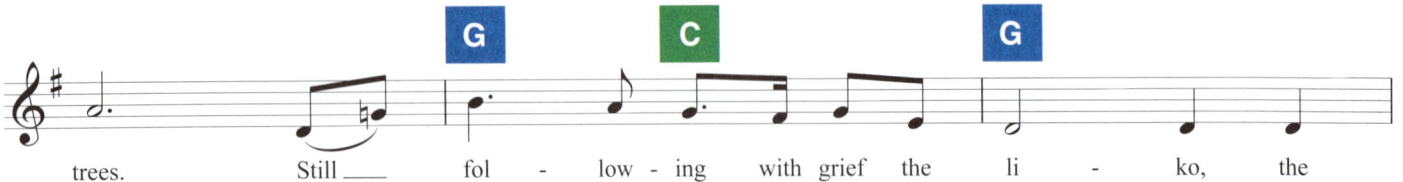
Proud-ly swept the rain cloud by the cliff as on it glid-ed through the

trees. Still fol-low-ing with grief the li-ko, the

a-mi-mi-le-mua of the vale. Fare-well to thee, fare-

well to thee, thou charm-ing one who dwells a-mong the bow-ers. One

fond em-brace be-fore I now de-part, un-til we meet a-gain.

Copyright © 2015 by HAL LEONARD CORPORATION
International Copyright Secured All Rights Reserved

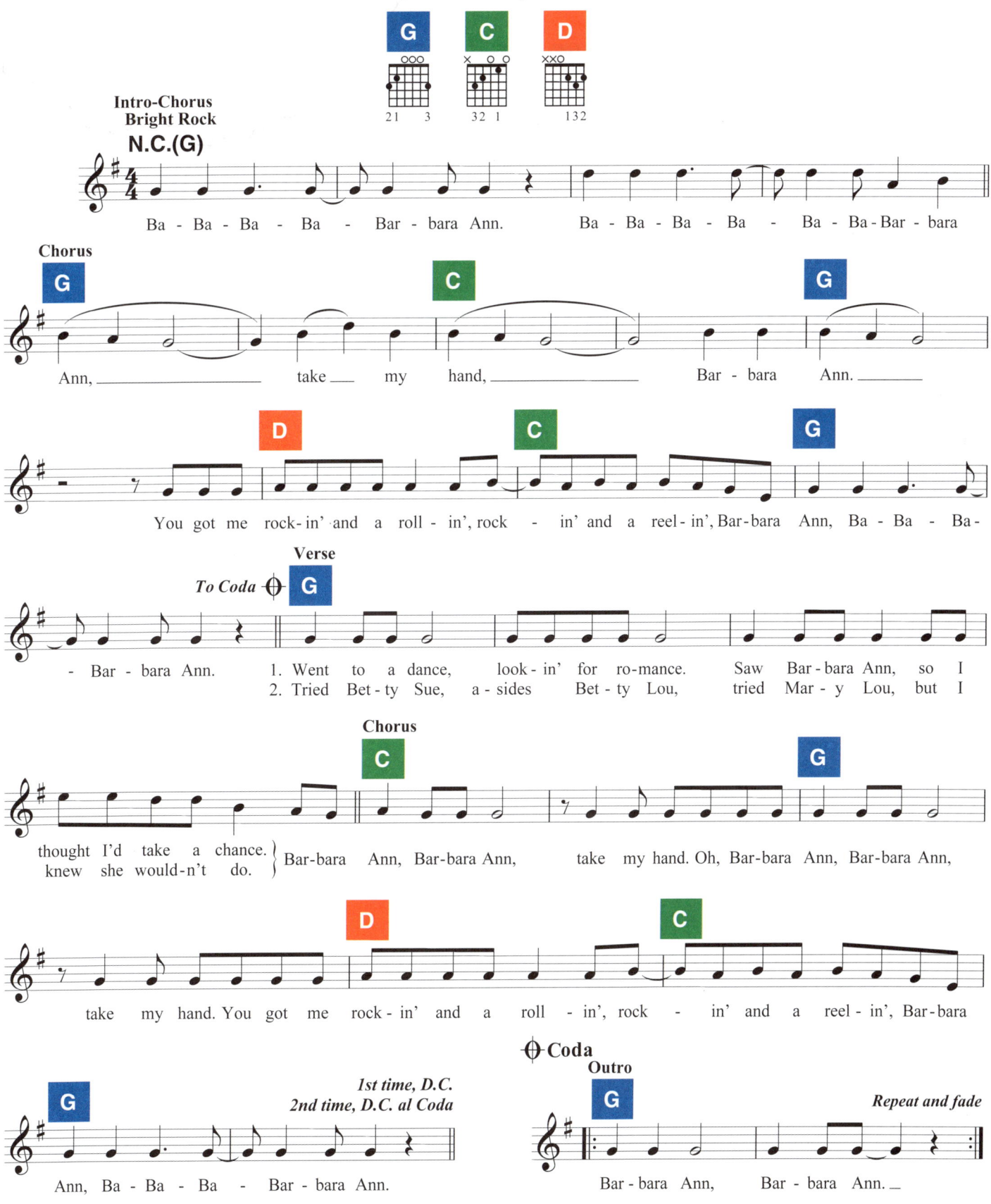

Amanda
Words and Music by Bob McDill

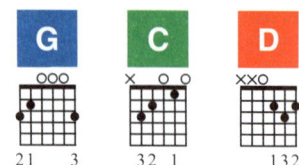

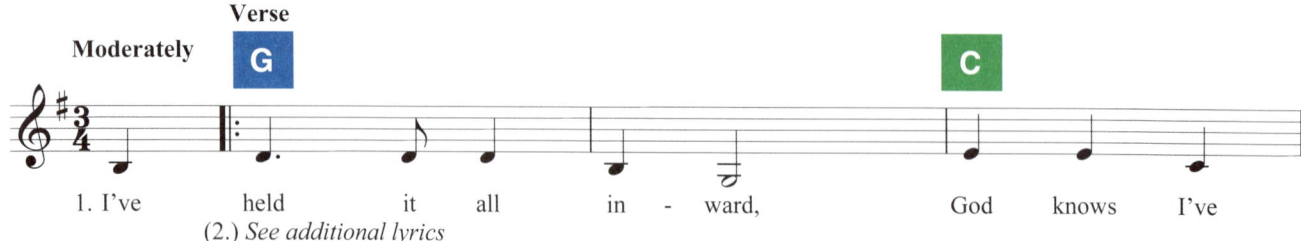
1. I've held it all in-ward, God knows I've
(2.) See additional lyrics

tried, but it's an awful awak-'ning in a

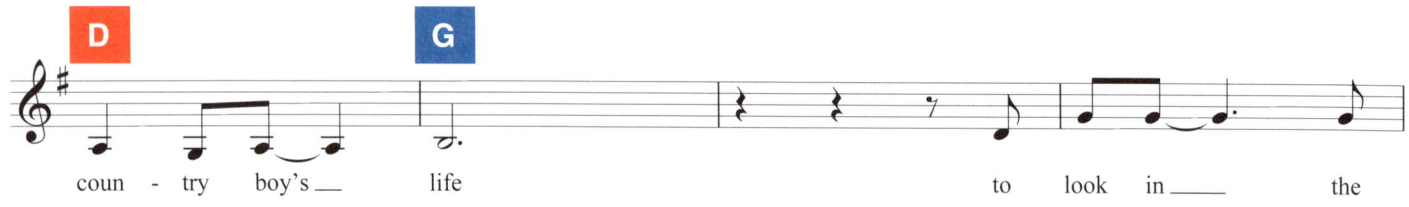
coun-try boy's life to look in the

mir-ror in to-tal sur-prise at the hair on my shoul-

Copyright © 1972, 1978 UNIVERSAL - SONGS OF POLYGRAM INTERNATIONAL, INC. and BOB McDILL MUSIC
Copyright Renewed
All Rights Controlled and Administered by UNIVERSAL - SONGS OF POLYGRAM INTERNATIONAL, INC.
All Rights Reserved   Used by Permission

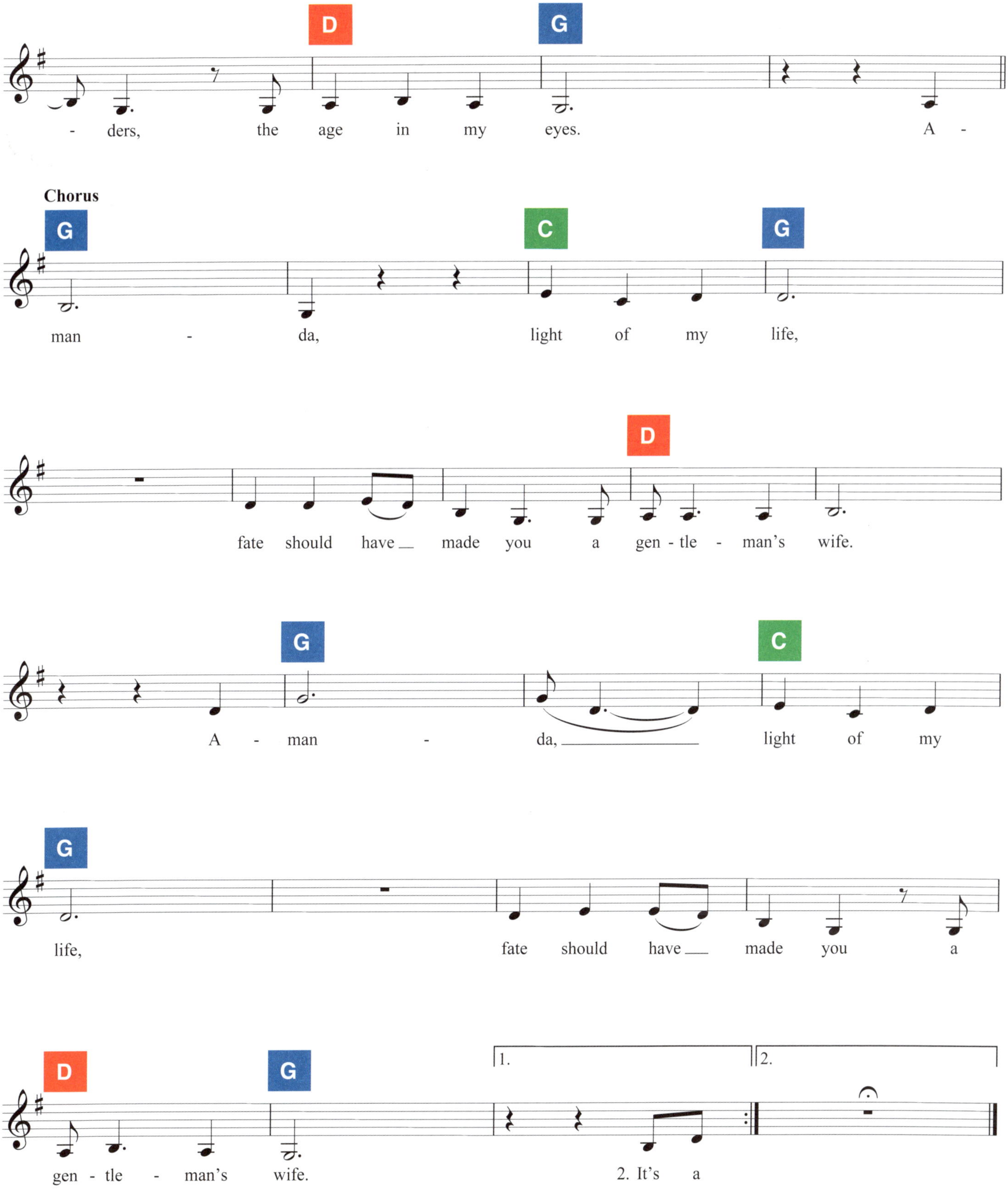

Additional Lyrics

2. It's a measure of people who don't understand
   The pleasures of life in a hillbilly band.
   I got my first guitar when I was fourteen.
   Well, I finally made forty, still wearing jeans.

Authority Song

Words and Music by John Mellencamp

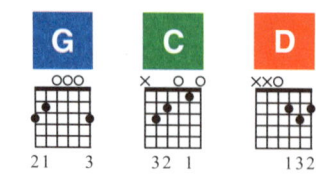

1. They ___ like to get you in a com-pro-mis-in' po-si-tion.
(2.) *See additional lyrics*

Yeah, they ___ like to get you there, ___ smile in your face. ___

Well, they think ___ they're so cute when they got you in that ___ con-di-

-tion, but I ___ think it's ___ a to-

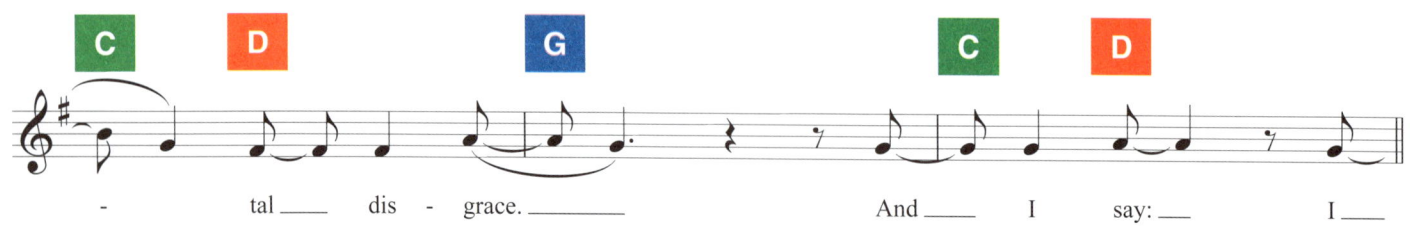

-tal ___ dis-grace. ___ And ___ I say: ___ I

© 1983 EMI FULL KEEL MUSIC
All Rights Reserved   International Copyright Secured   Used by Permission

Additional Lyrics

2. I call up my preacher. I say, "Give me strength for Round Five."
He said, "You don't need no strength. You need to grow up, son."
I say, "Growin' up leads to growin' old and then dyin'.
And dyin', to me, don't sound like all that much fun."
So I say:

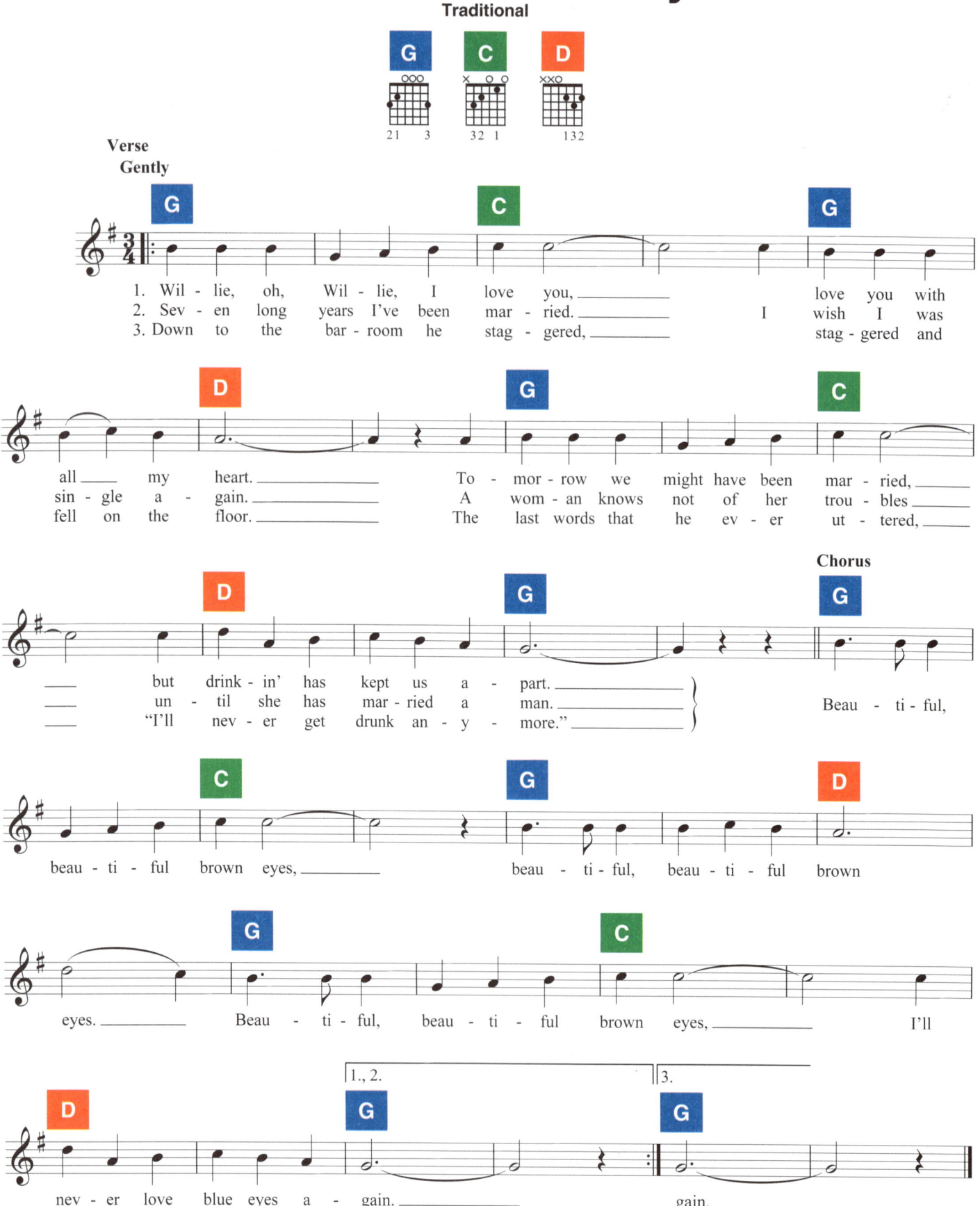

Blue Moon of Kentucky
Words and Music by Bill Monroe

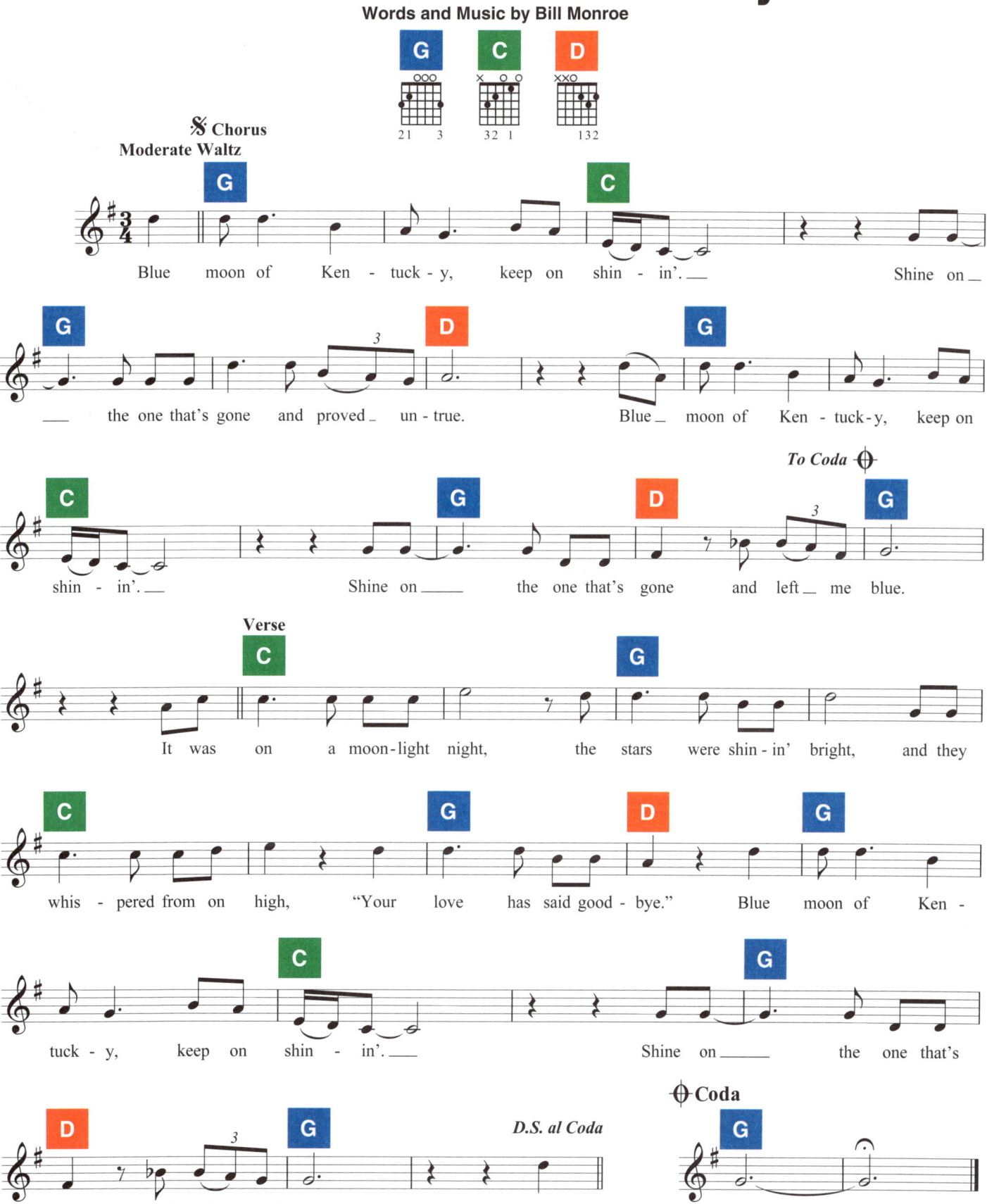

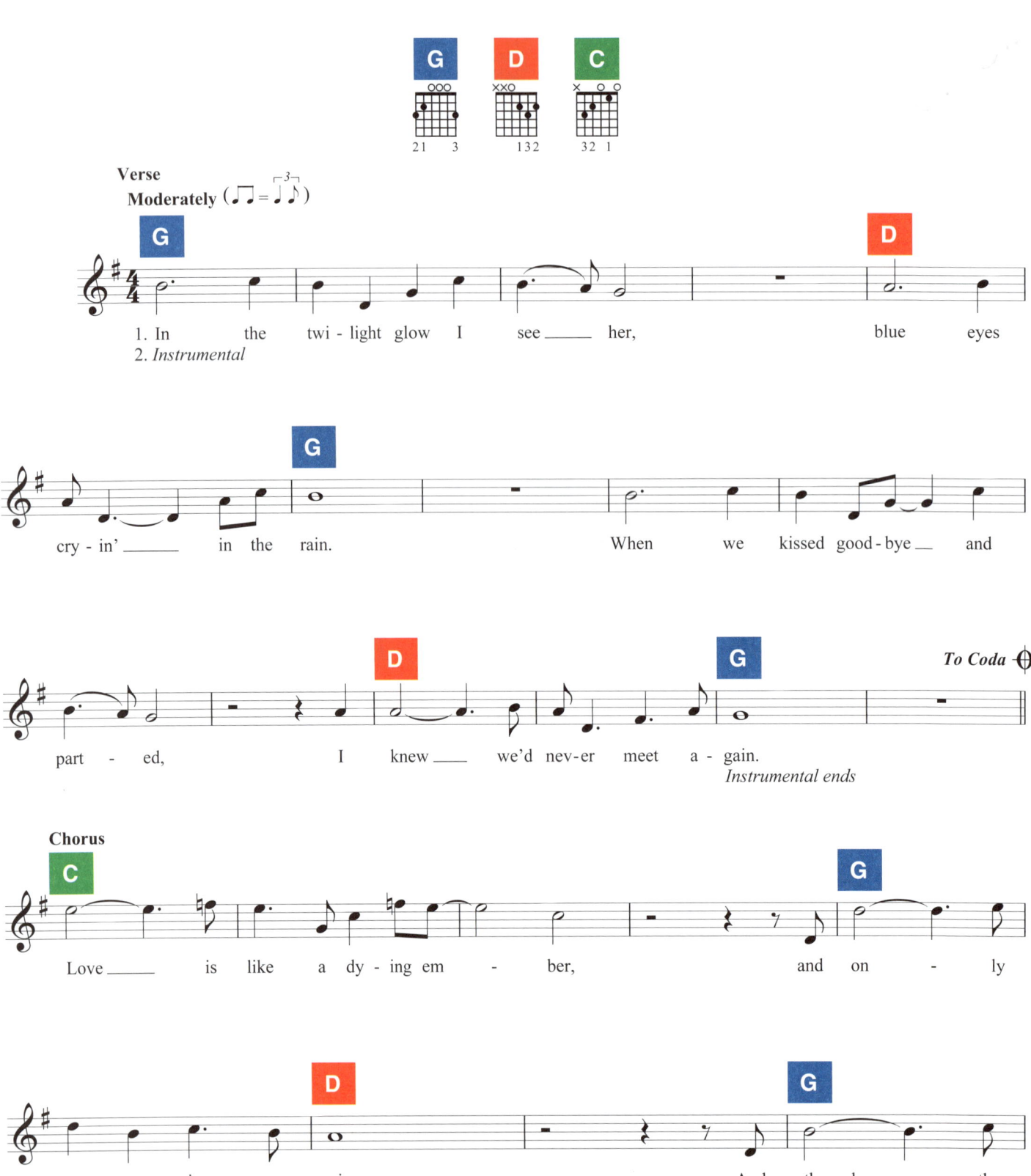

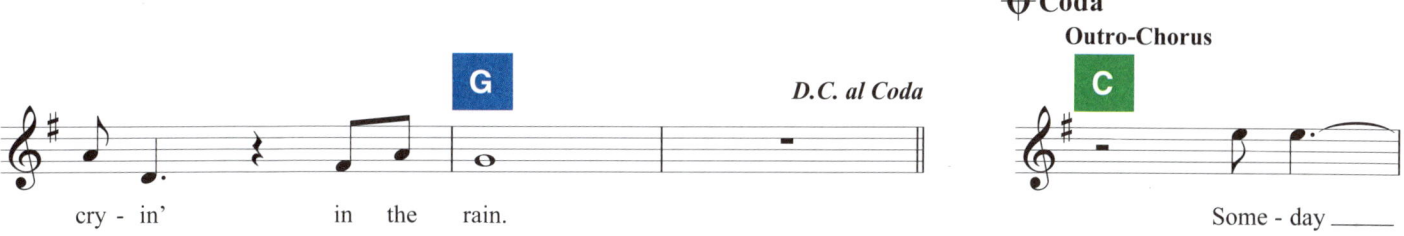

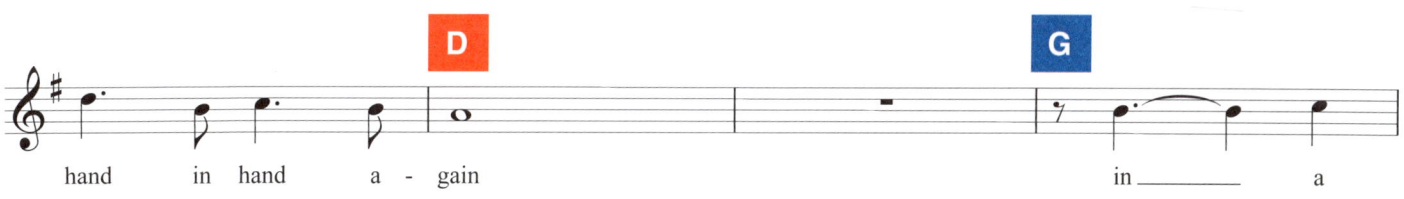

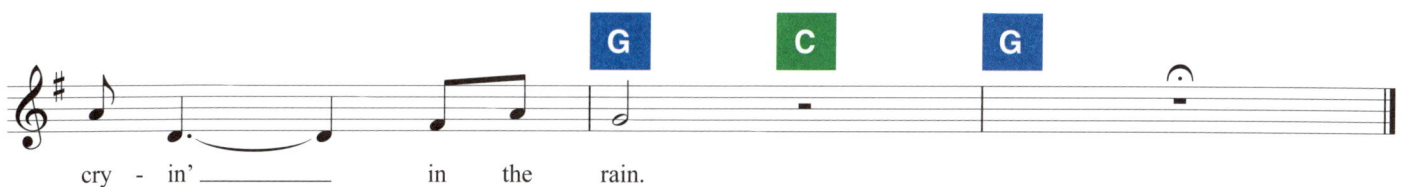

The Blue Tail Fly
(Jimmy Crack Corn)
Words and Music by Daniel Decatur Emmett

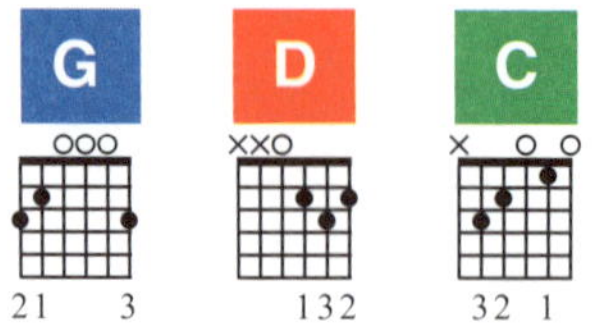

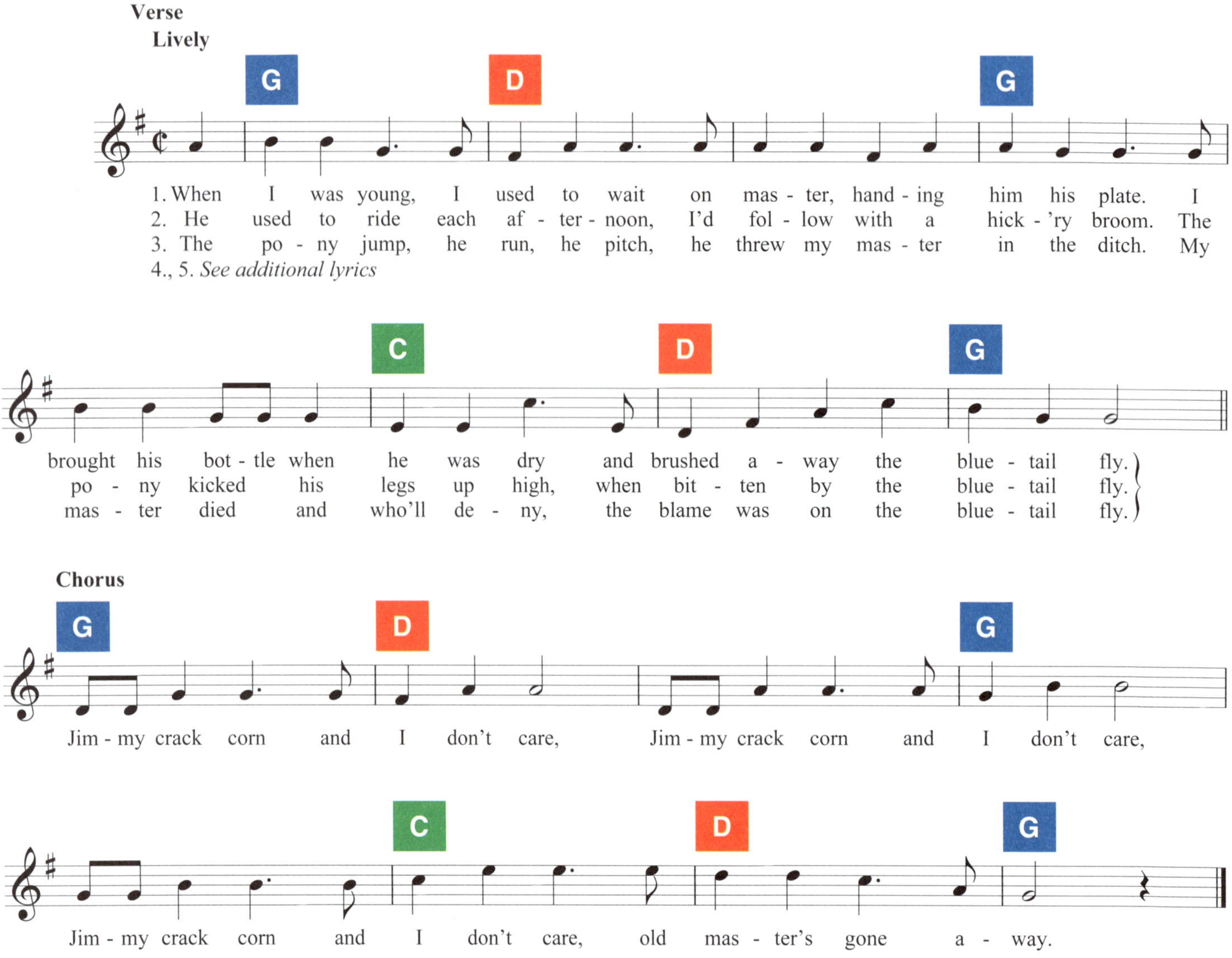

Verse
Lively

1. When I was young, I used to wait on mas-ter, hand-ing him his plate. I
2. He used to ride each af-ter-noon, I'd fol-low with a hick-'ry broom. The
3. The po-ny jump, he run, he pitch, he threw my mas-ter in the ditch. My
4., 5. *See additional lyrics*

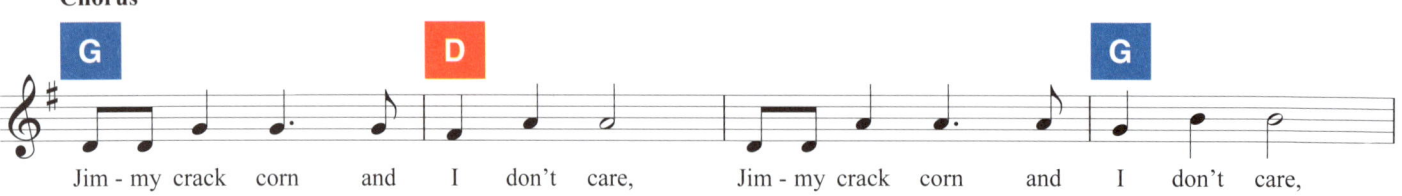

brought his bot-tle when he was dry and brushed a-way the blue-tail fly.
po-ny kicked his legs up high, when bit-ten by the blue-tail fly.
mas-ter died and who'll de-ny, the blame was on the blue-tail fly.

Chorus

Jim-my crack corn and I don't care, Jim-my crack corn and I don't care,

Jim-my crack corn and I don't care, old mas-ter's gone a-way.

Additional Lyrics

4. Old master's dead and gone to rest,
   They say it happened for the best.
   I won't forget until I die
   My master and the blue-tail fly.

5. A skeeter bites right through your clothes,
   A hornet strikes you on the nose,
   The bees may get you passing by,
   But, oh, much worse, the blue-tail fly.

Copyright © 2015 by HAL LEONARD CORPORATION
International Copyright Secured   All Rights Reserved

Cindy

Southern Appalachian Folksong

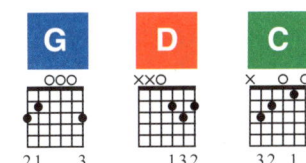

Verse
Quickly

1. You ought to see my Cindy, she lives a-way down
2. I wish I was an apple a-hangin' on a
3. I wish I had a needle as fine as I could

4., 5. *See additional lyrics*

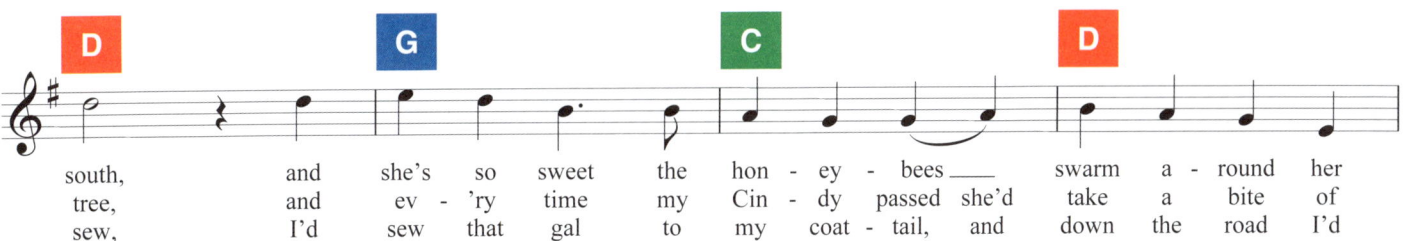

south, and she's so sweet the honey-bees swarm a-round her
tree, and ev'ry time my Cindy passed she'd take a bite of
sew, I'd sew that gal to my coat-tail, and down the road I'd

Chorus

mouth.
me. } Get a-long home, Cin-dy, Cin-dy. Get a-long home, Cin-dy,
go.

Cin-dy. Get a-long home, Cin-dy, Cin-dy. I'll mar-ry you some-day.

Additional Lyrics

4. I wish I had a nickel,
   I wish I had a dime,
   I wish I had my Cindy girl
   To love me all the time.

5. Cindy in the springtime,
   Cindy in the fall;
   If I can't have my Cindy,
   I'll have no girl at all.

Copyright © 2015 by HAL LEONARD CORPORATION
International Copyright Secured   All Rights Reserved

Boot Scootin' Boogie

Words and Music by Ronnie Dunn

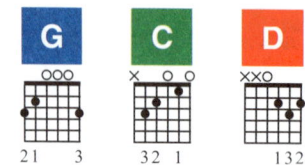

Verse
Moderately

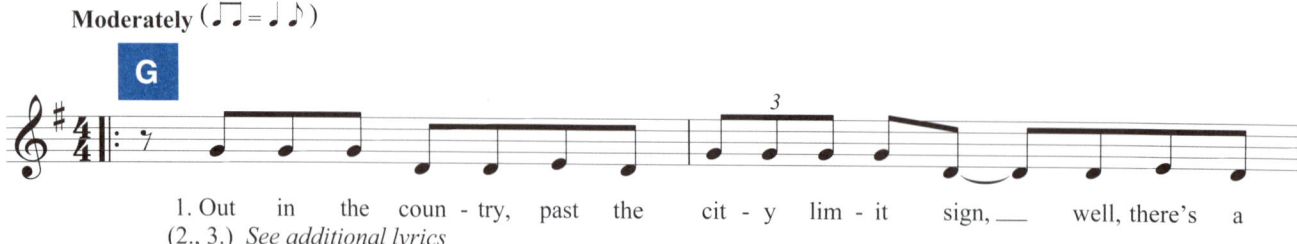

1. Out in the coun-try, past the cit-y lim-it sign,___ well, there's a
(2., 3.) *See additional lyrics*

hon-ky-tonk___ near the coun-ty line.___ The joint starts jump-in' ev-'ry

night when the sun___ goes down.___ They got whis-

-key, wom-en,___ mu-sic and smoke.___ It's where all the cow-boy folk___

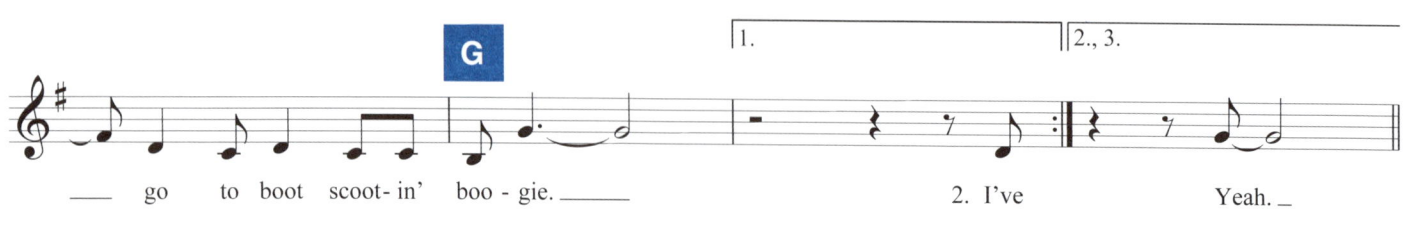

___ go to boot scoot-in' boo-gie.___ 2. I've Yeah.___

Copyright © 1991 Sony/ATV Music Publishing LLC
All Rights Administered by Sony/ATV Music Publishing LLC, 424 Church Street, Suite 1200, Nashville, TN 37219
International Copyright Secured   All Rights Reserved

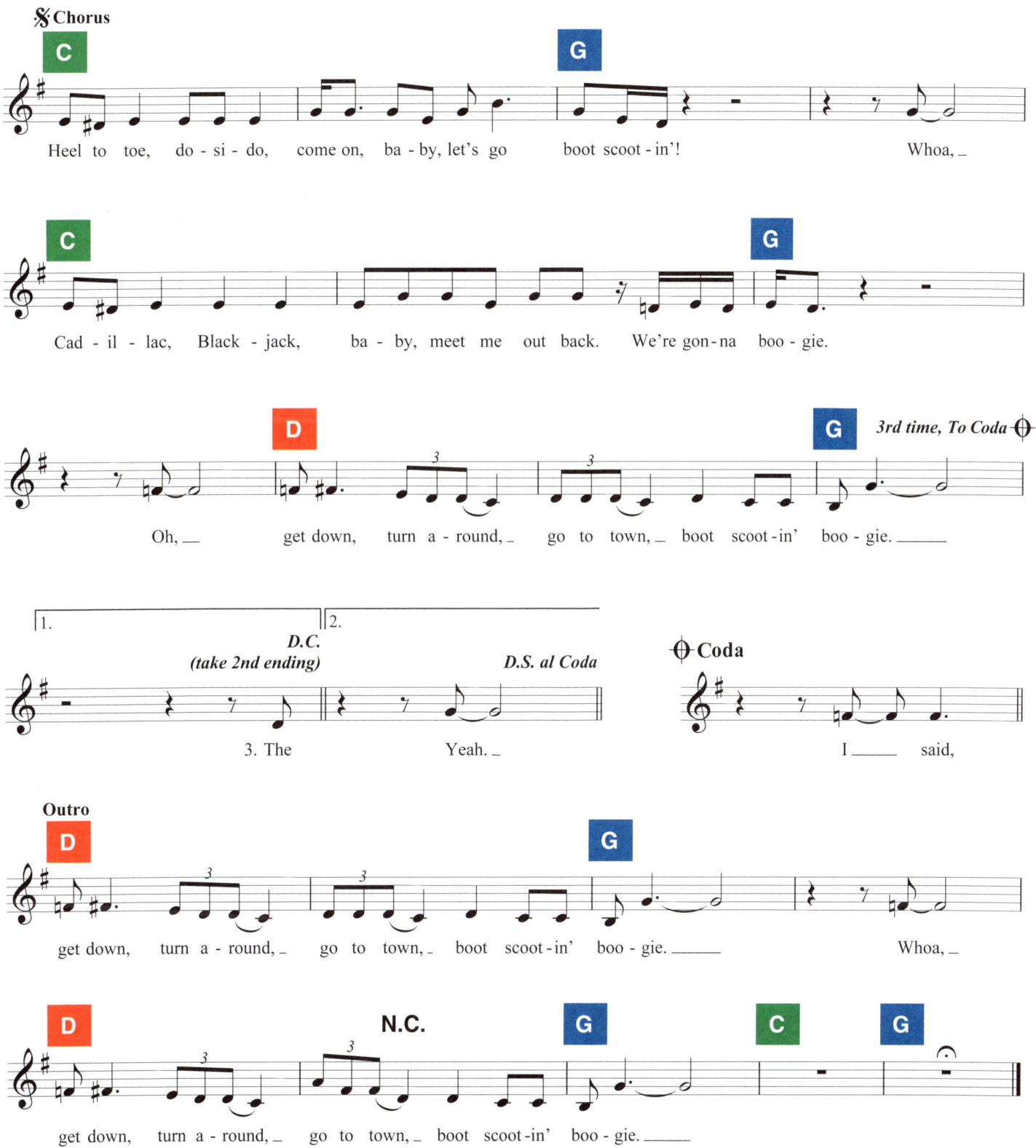

Additional Lyrics

2. I've got a good job, I work hard for my money.
   When it's quittin' time, I hit the door runnin'.
   I fire up my pickup truck and let the horses run.
   I go flyin' down that highway to that hideaway
   Stuck out in the woods, to do the boot scootin' boogie.

3. The bartender asks me, says, "Son, what will it be?"
   I want a shot at that red-head yonder lookin' at me.
   The dance floor's hoppin' and it's hotter than the Fourth of July.
   I see outlaws, in-laws, crooks and straights,
   All out makin' it shake, doin' the boot scootin' boogie.

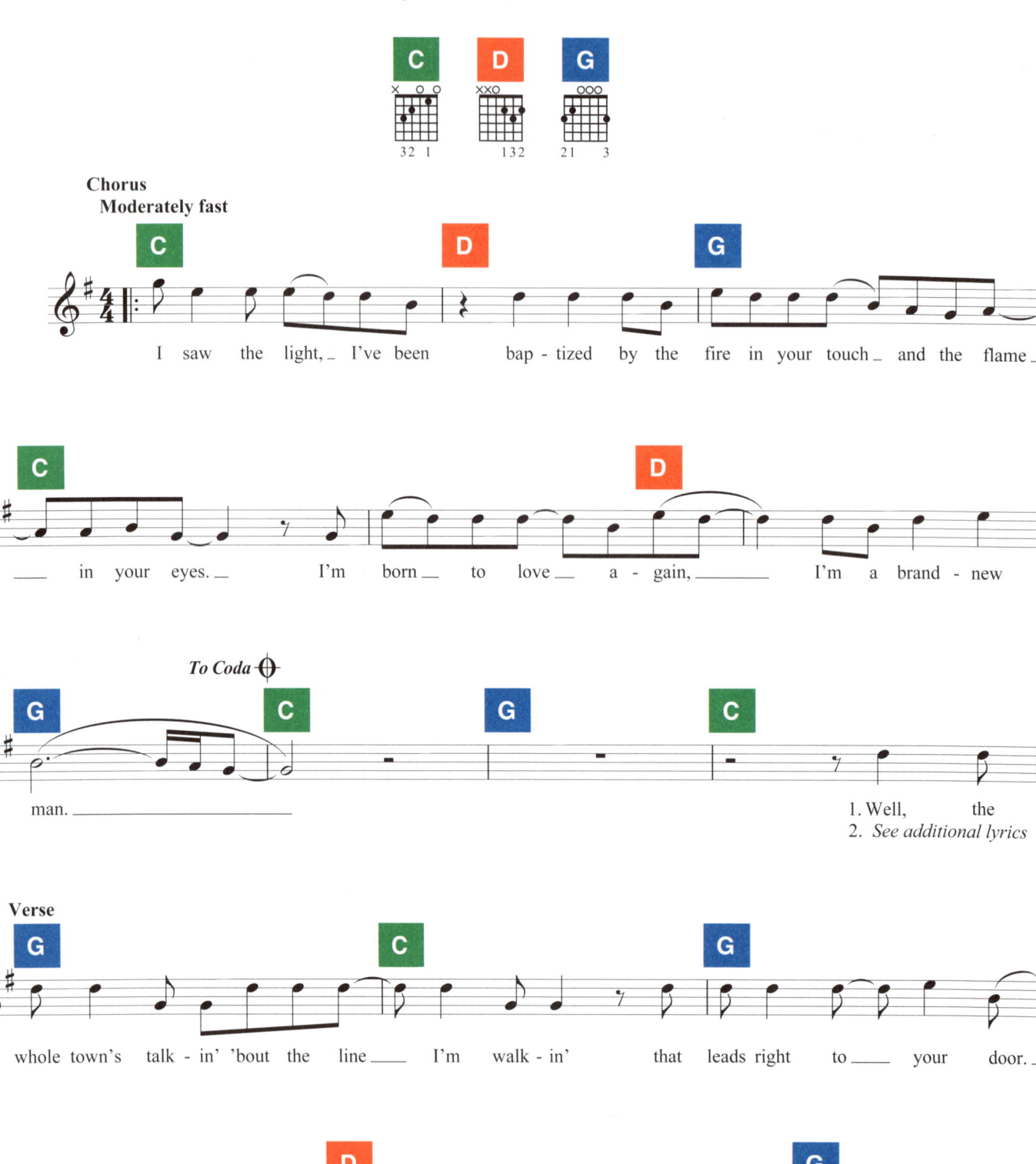

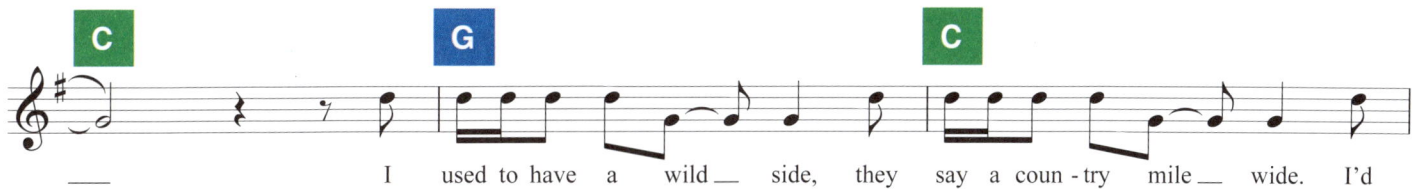
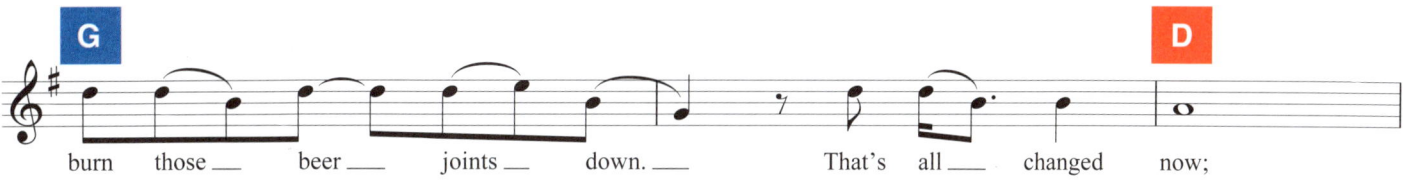

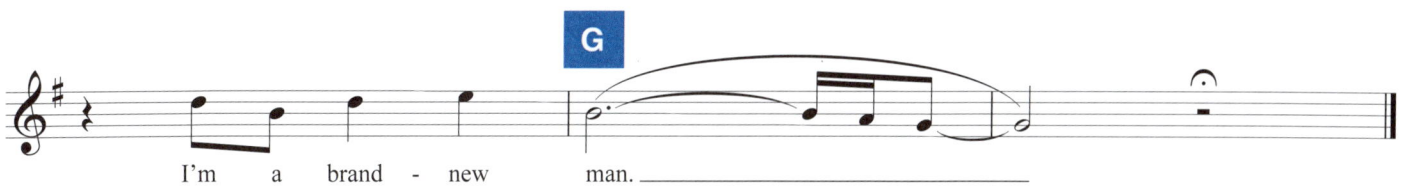

Additional Lyrics

2. I used to love 'em and leave 'em, oh, I'd brag about my freedom,
How no one could tie me down.
Then I met you; now my heart beats true.
Baby, you and me together feels more like forever
Than anything I've ever known.
We're right on track. I ain't lookin' back.

Call Me the Breeze

Words and Music by John Cale

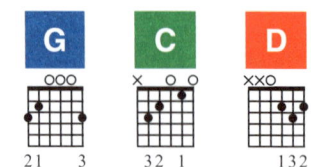

Chorus
Moderately fast

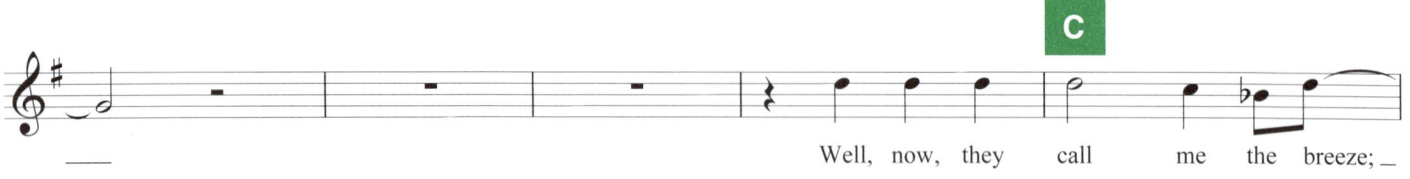

Call, call me the breeze; I keep blow-in' down the road.

Well, now, they call me the breeze;

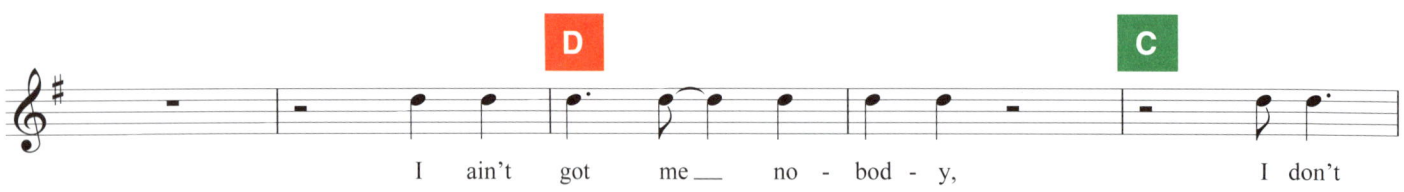

I keep blow-in' down the road.

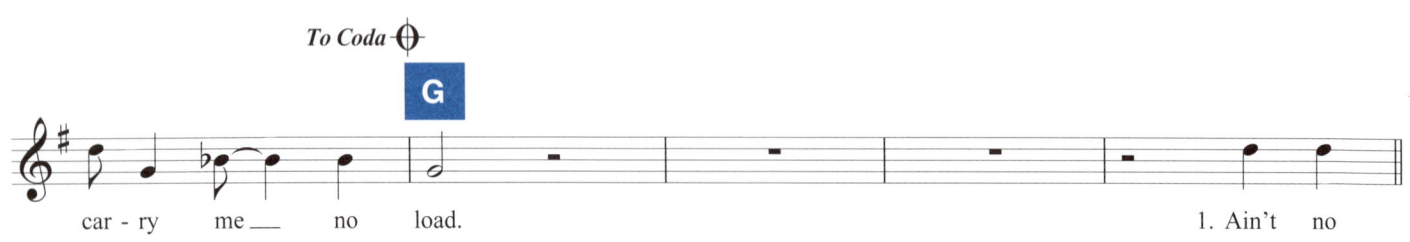

I ain't got me nobody, I don't carry me no load. 1. Ain't no

Copyright © 1971 by Johnny Bienstock Music
Copyright Renewed
International Copyright Secured All Rights Reserved
Used by Permission

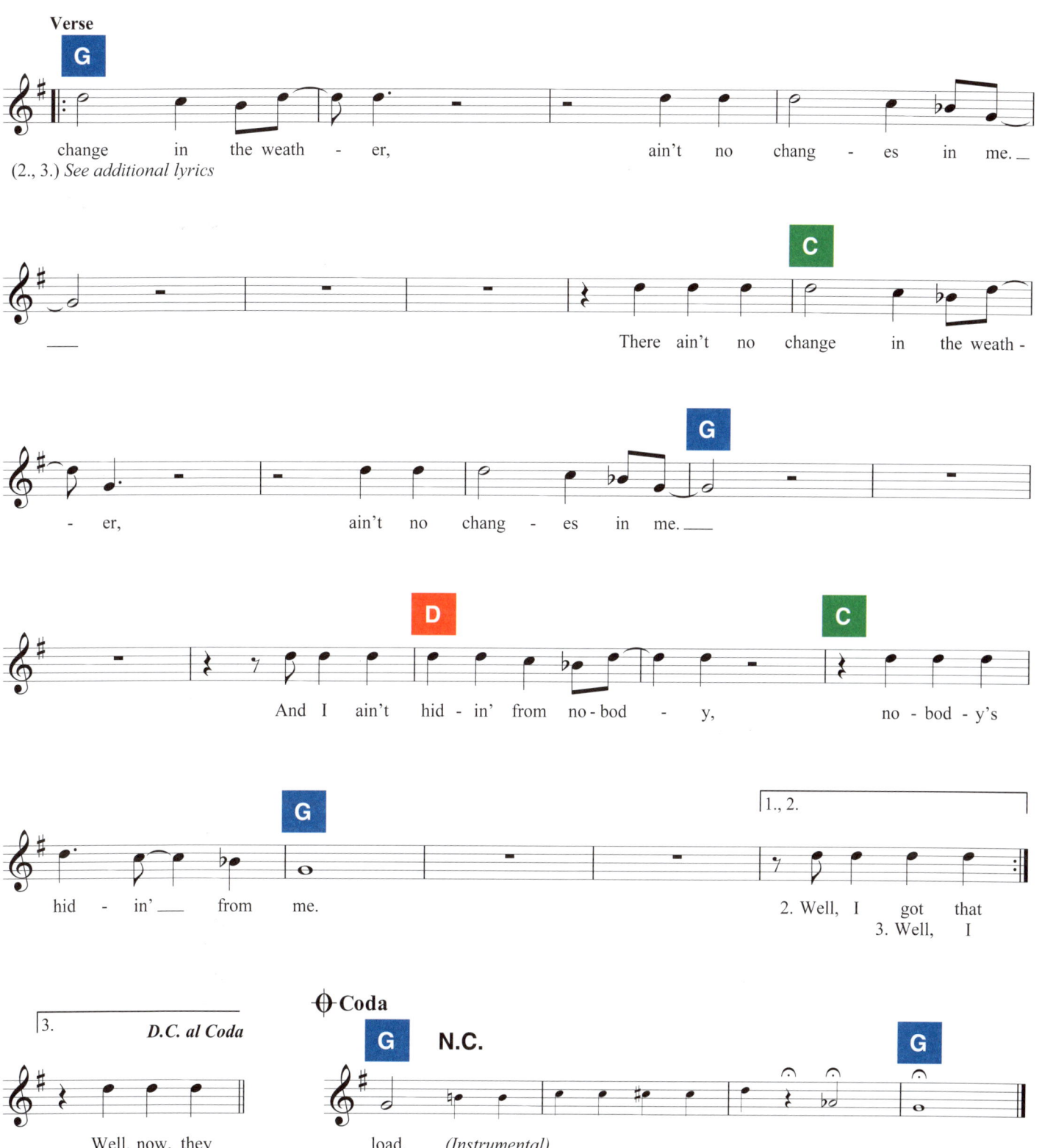

Additional Lyrics

2. Well, I got that green light, baby; I got to keep movin' on.
   Well, I got that green light, baby; I got to keep movin' on.
   Well, I might go out to California, might go down to Georgia, I don't know.

3. Well, I dig you Georgia peaches; makes me feel right at home.
   Well, now, I dig you Georgia peaches; makes me feel right at home.
   But I don't love me no one woman, so I can't stay in Georgia long.

Chantilly Lace

Words and Music by J.P. Richardson

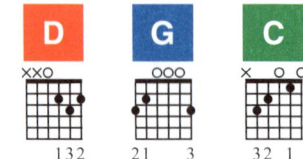

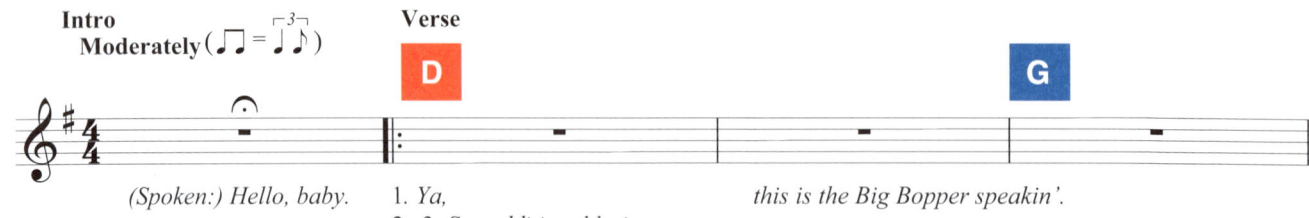

(Spoken:) Hello, baby. 1. Ya, this is the Big Bopper speakin'.
2., 3. See additional lyrics

Ha, ha, ha, ha, ha, ha. Oh, you sweet thing!

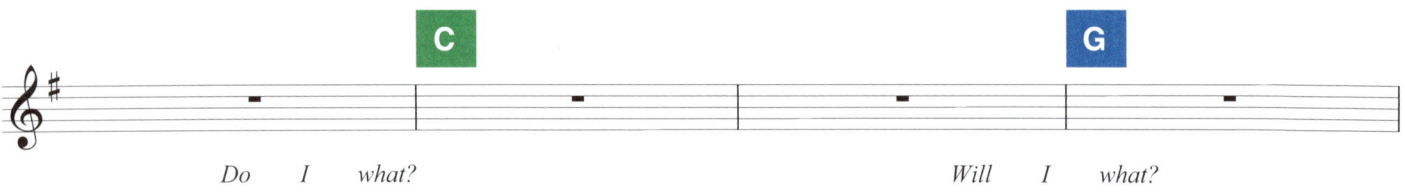

Do I what? Will I what?

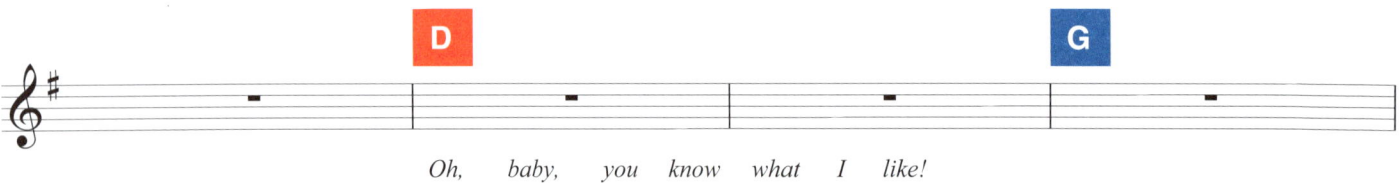

Oh, baby, you know what I like!

Chan-til-ly lace___ and a pret-ty face___ and a po-ny-tail___

Copyright © 1958 by Fort Knox Music Inc., Trio Music Company and Glad Music Co.
Copyright Renewed
All Rights for Trio Music Company Controlled and Administered by BUG Music, Inc., a BMG Chrysalis company
International Copyright Secured   All Rights Reserved
Used by Permission

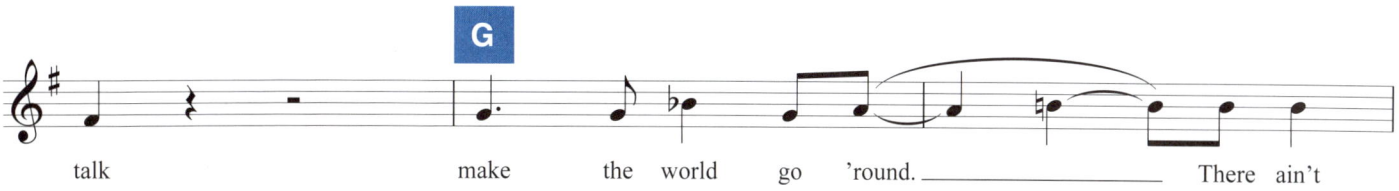

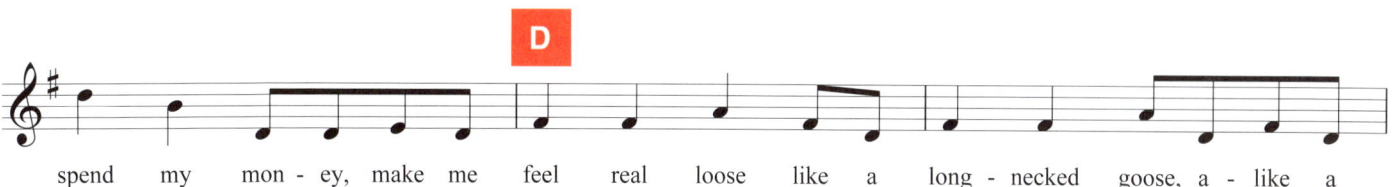

Additional Lyrics

2. *(Spoken:)* What's that, baby?
   But, but, but,
   Oh, honey,
   But, oh baby, you know what I like!

3. *(Spoken:)* What's that, honey?
   Pick you up at eight, and don't be late?
   But, baby, I ain't got no money, honey!
   Ha, ha, ha, ha, ha.
   Oh, alright, honey, you know what I like!

Cherry, Cherry

Words and Music by Neil Diamond

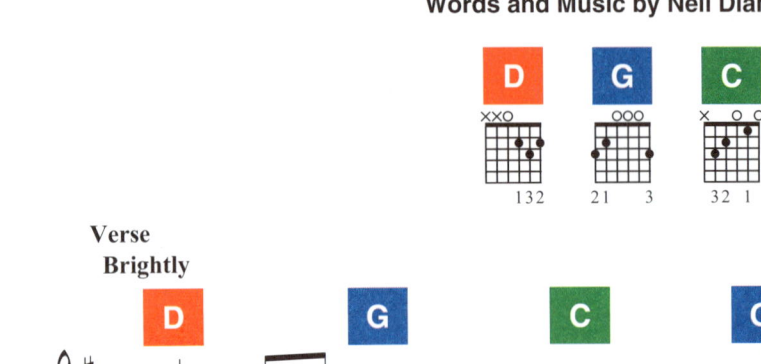

1. Ba-by loves me, yes, yes, she does.
2. Y'ain't got no right, no, no, you don't,

Ah, the girl's out-ta sight, yeah.
ah, to be so ex-cit-ing.

Says she loves me, yes, yes, she does.
Won't need bright lights, no, no, we won't.

Gon-na show me to-night, yeah.
Gon-na make our own light-ning.

Chorus

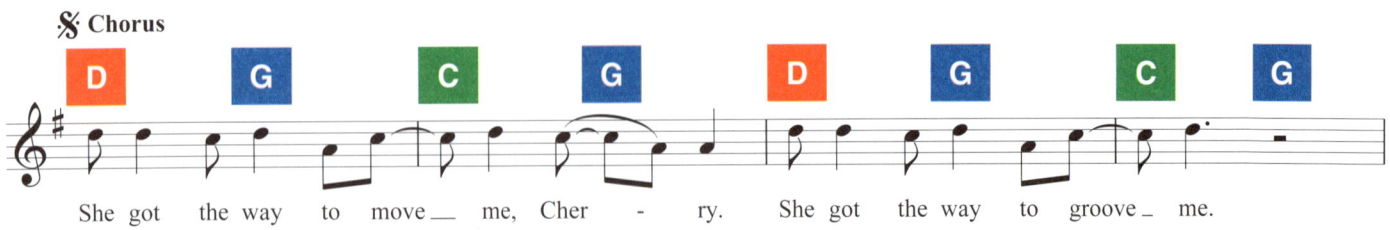

She got the way to move me, Cher-ry. She got the way to groove me.

Closer to Free

Words and Music by Sam Llanas and Kurt Neumann

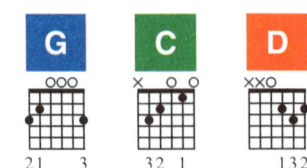

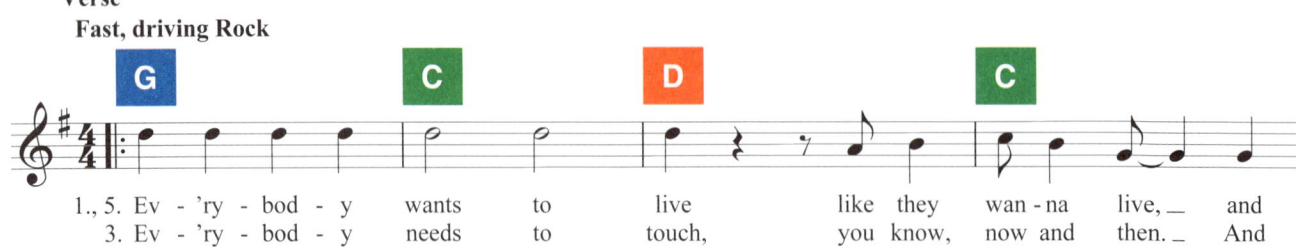

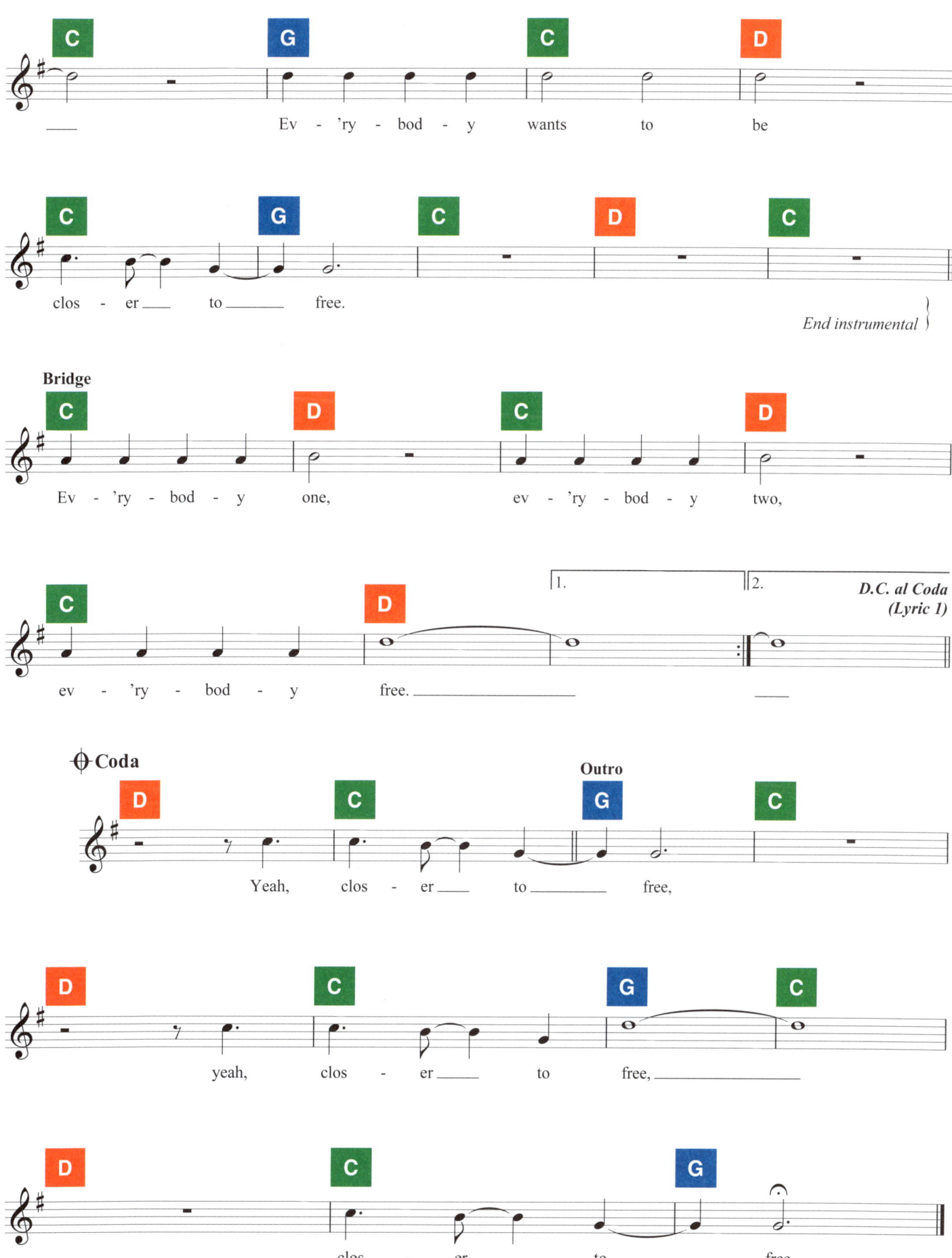

Cockles and Mussels
(Molly Malone)
Traditional Irish Folksong

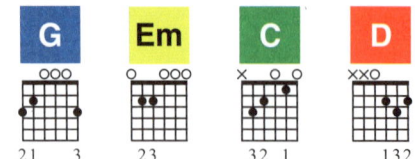

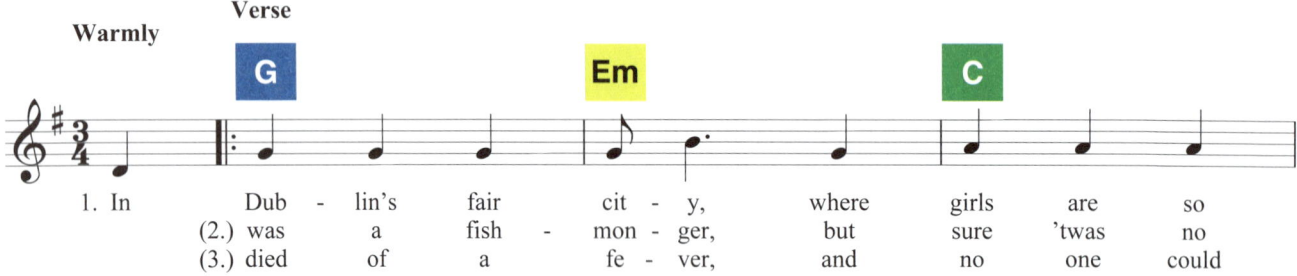

Copyright © 2015 by HAL LEONARD CORPORATION
International Copyright Secured   All Rights Reserved

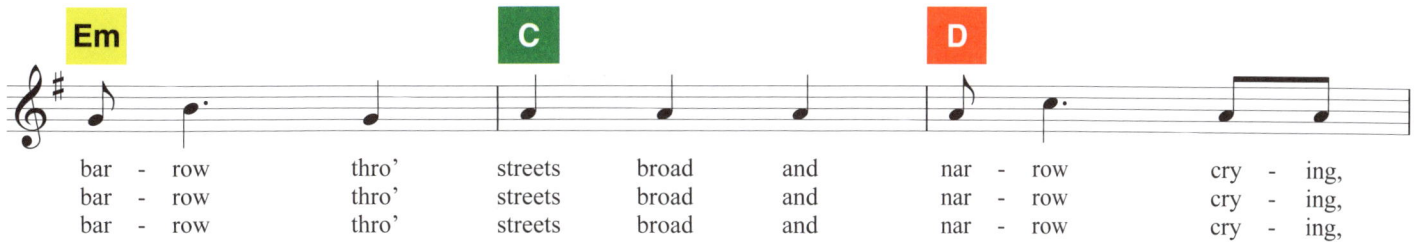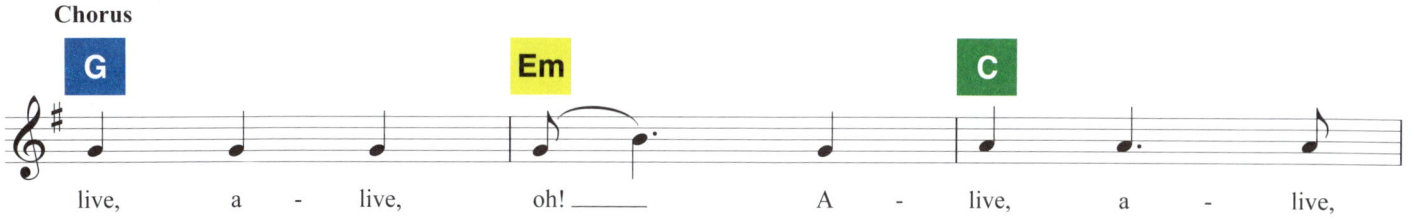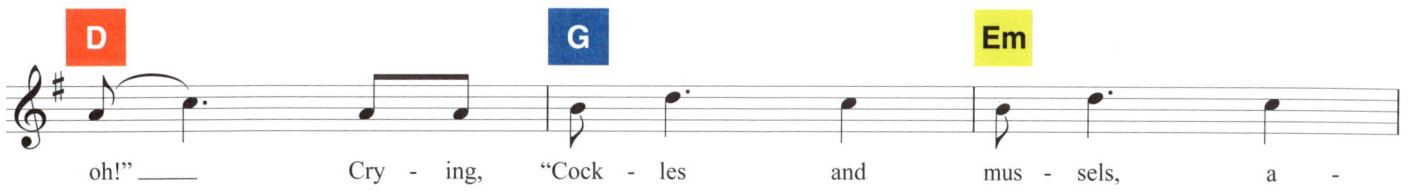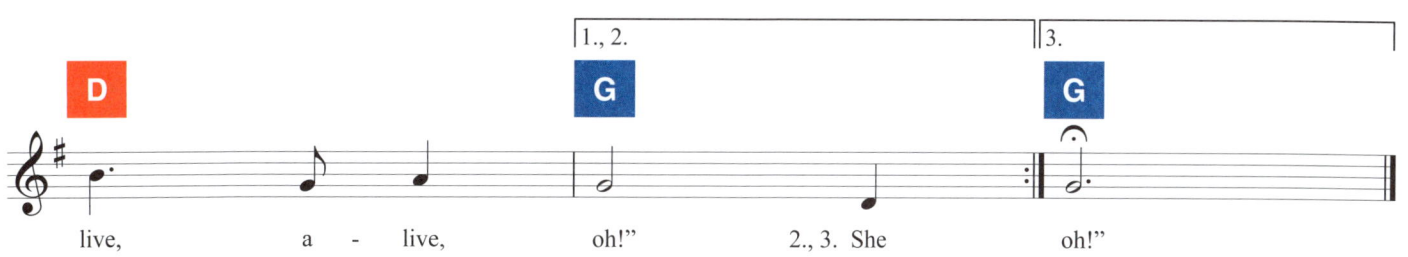

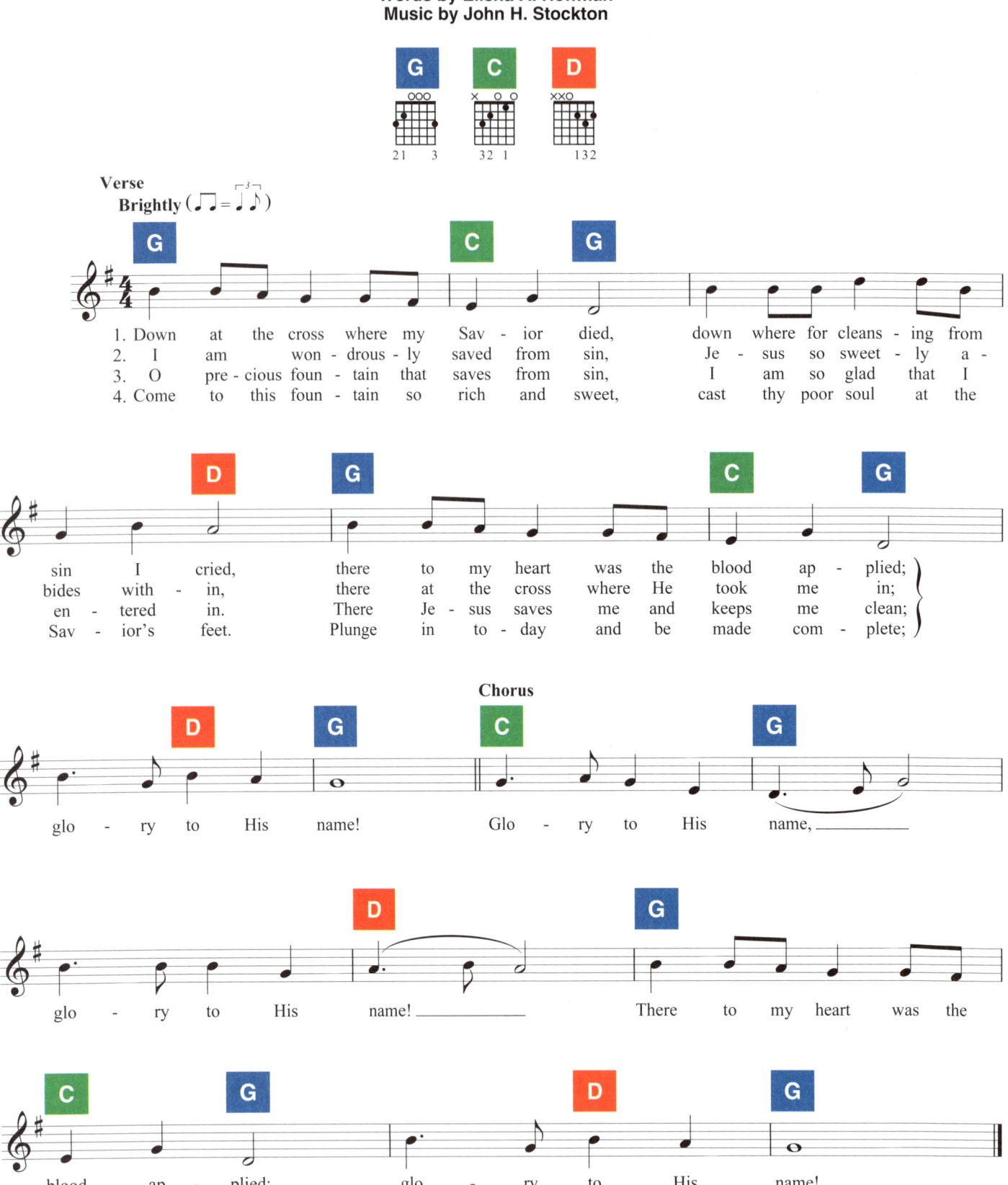

Have You Ever Seen the Rain?

Words and Music by John Fogerty

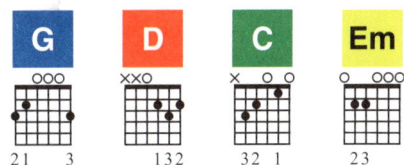

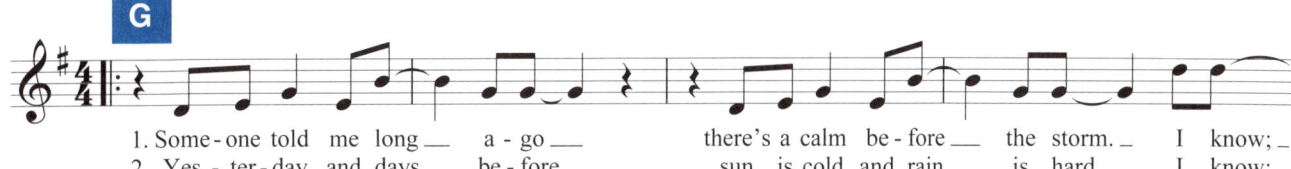

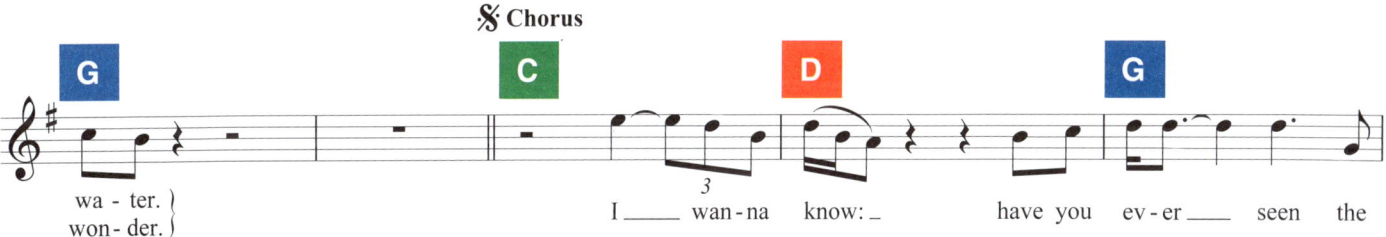

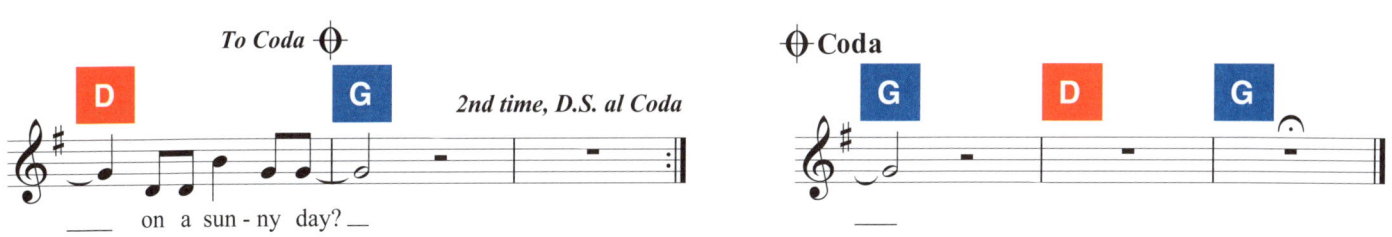

Copyright © 1970 Jondora Music
Copyright Renewed
International Copyright Secured All Rights Reserved

Early Mornin' Rain

Words and Music by Gordon Lightfoot

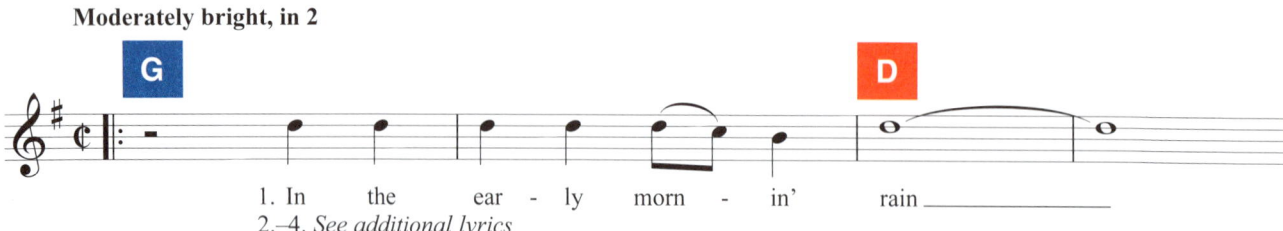

1. In the ear - ly morn - in' rain
2.–4. *See additional lyrics*

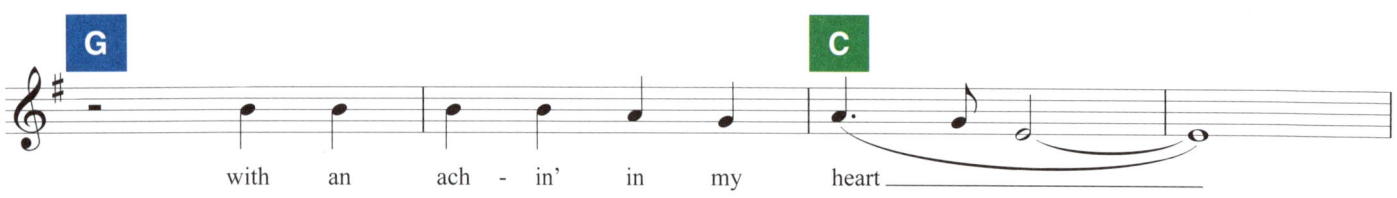
with a dol - lar in my hand,

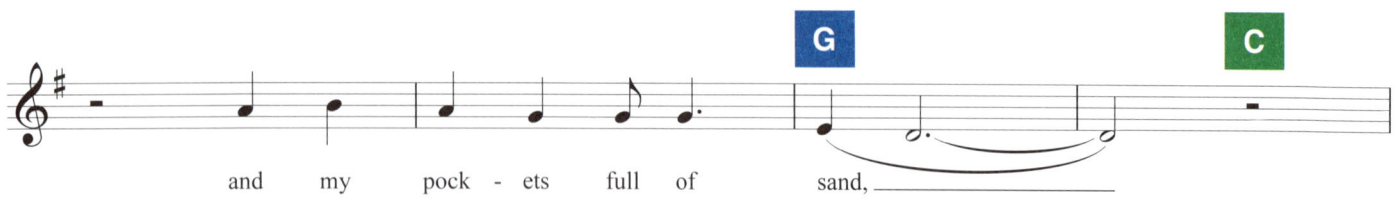
with an ach - in' in my heart

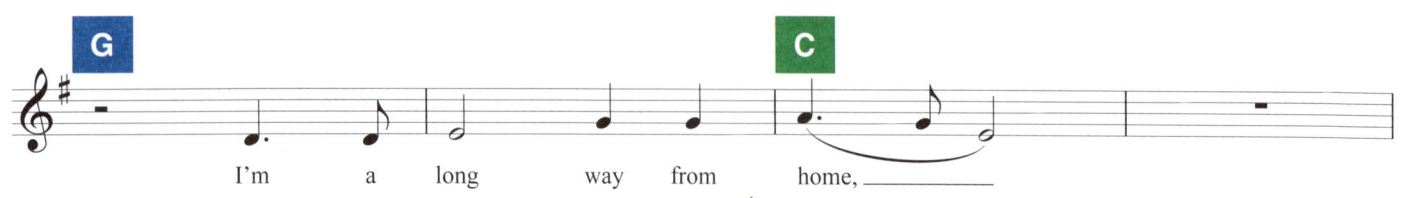
and my pock - ets full of sand,

I'm a long way from home,

© 1965 (Renewed) WB MUSIC CORP.
All Rights Reserved   Used by Permission

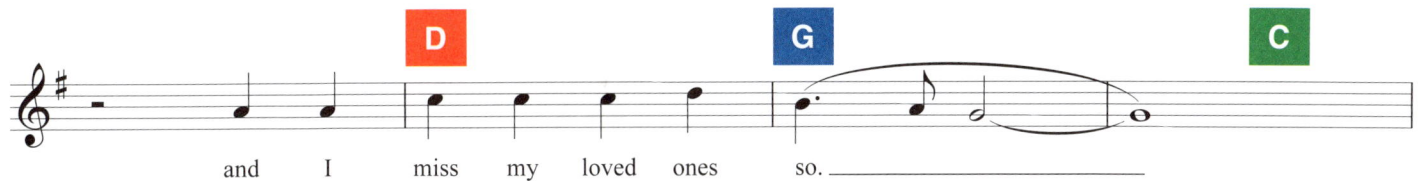

Additional Lyrics

2. Out on runway number nine,
   Big 707 set to go.
   But I'm stuck here in the grass
   Where the cold wind blows.
   Now the liquor tasted good,
   And the women all were fast.
   Well, there she goes, my friend,
   She's rollin' now at last.

3. Hear the mighty engines roar,
   See the silver bird on high.
   She's away and westward bound,
   Far above the clouds she'll fly,
   Where the mornin' rain don't fall
   And the sun always shines.
   She'll be flyin' o'er my home
   In about three hours' time.

4. This old airport's got me down;
   It's no earthly good to me.
   'Cause I'm stuck here on the ground,
   As cold and drunk as I can be.
   You can't jump a jet plane
   Like you can a freight train,
   So I'd best be on my way
   In the early mornin' rain.

Every Rose Has Its Thorn

Words and Music by Bobby Dall, C.C. Deville, Bret Michaels and Rikki Rockett

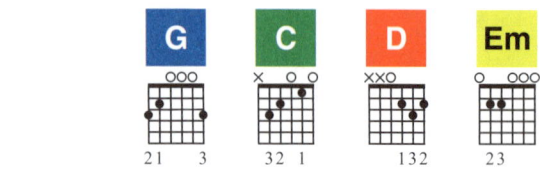

Verse
Moderately slow

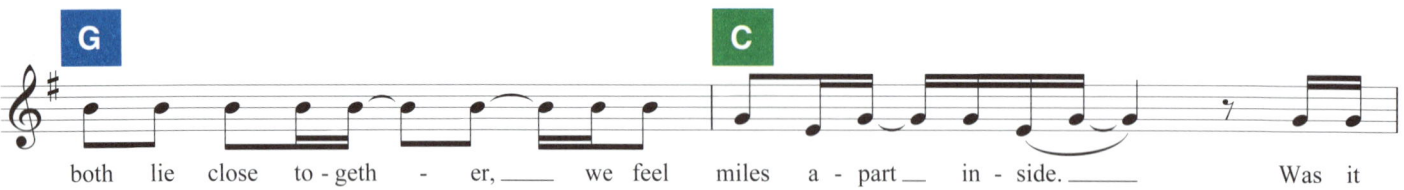

1. We both lie si-lent-ly still in the dead of the night. Al-though we
2., 3. *See additional lyrics*

both lie close to-geth - er, we feel miles a-part in - side. Was it

some-thing I said or some-thing I did? Did my words not come out right? Though I

Chorus

tried not to hurt you, though I tried, but I guess that's why they say ev-'ry rose has its

thorn, just like ev-'ry night has its dawn. Just like

Copyright © 1988 by Cyanide Publishing
All Rights in the United States Administered by Universal Music - Z Songs
International Copyright Secured   All Rights Reserved

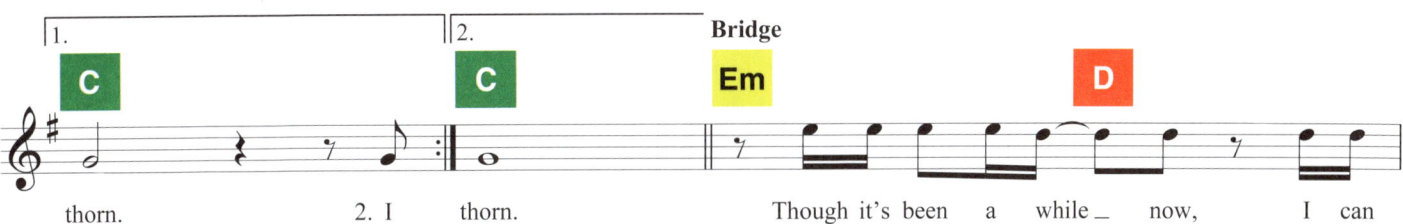
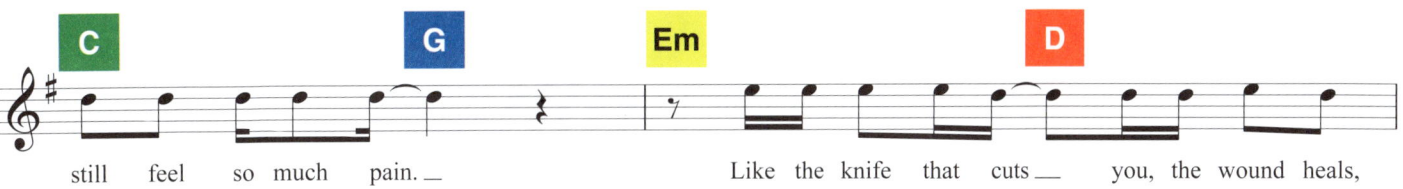
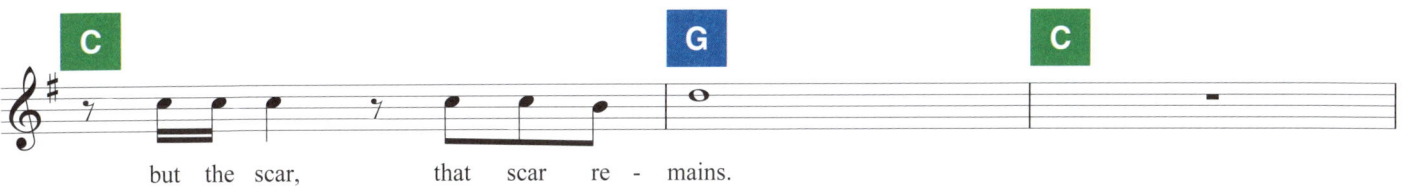
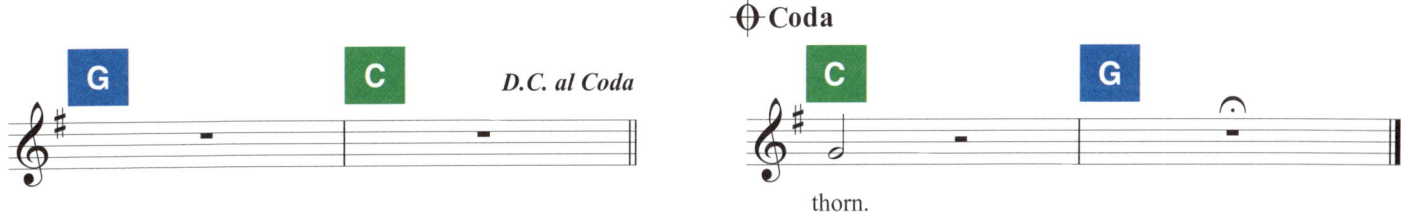

Additional Lyrics

2. I listen to our favorite song playing on the radio,
   Hear the DJ say love's a game of easy come and easy go.
   But I wonder, does he know? Has he ever felt like this?
   And I know that you'd be here right now if I could've let you know somehow.
   I guess... *(To Chorus)*

3. I know I could have saved our love that night if I'd known what to say.
   Instead of making love, we both made our separate ways.
   And now I hear you've found somebody new and that I never meant that much to you.
   To hear that tears me up inside and to see you cuts me like a knife.
   I guess... *(To Chorus)*

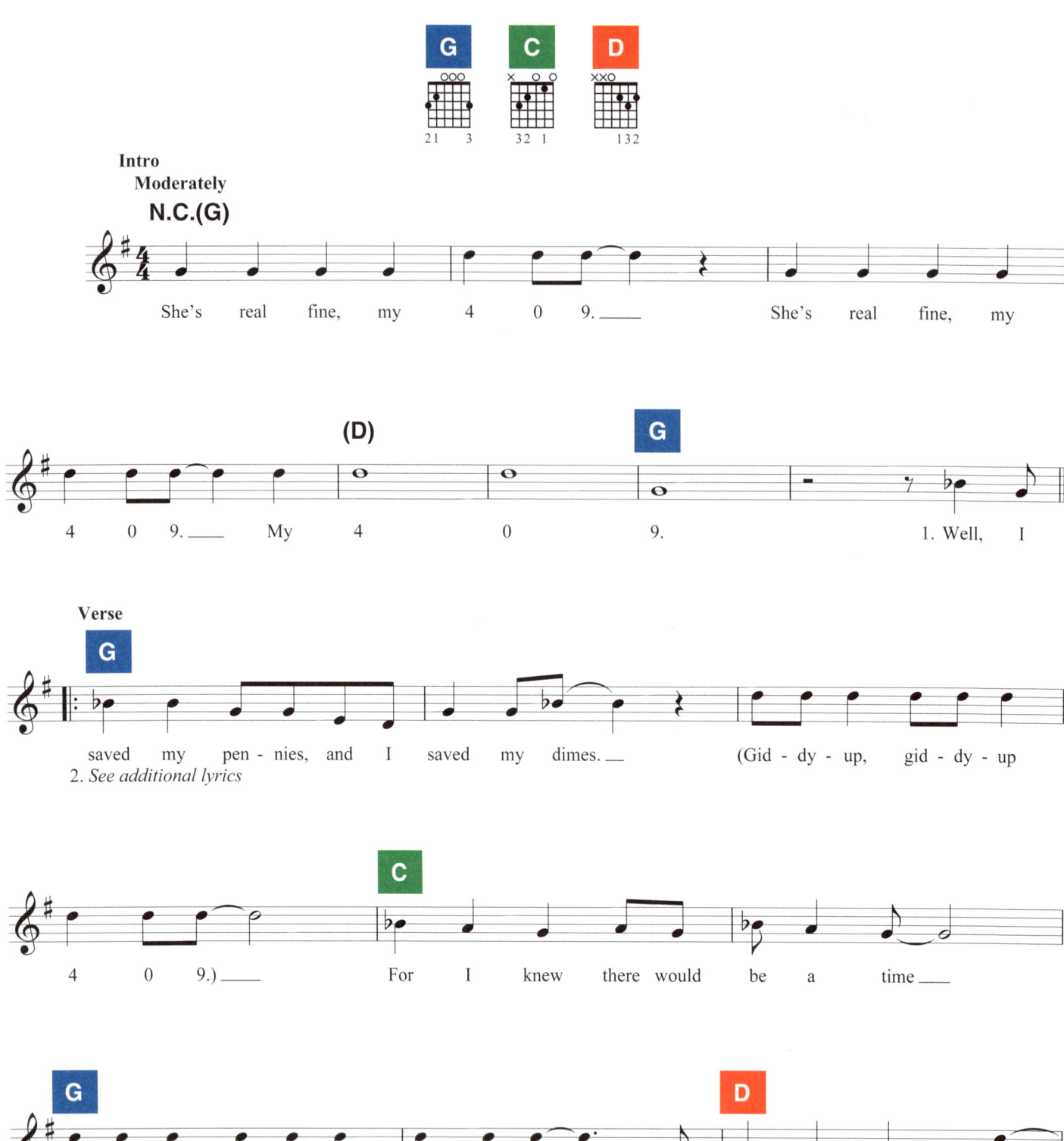

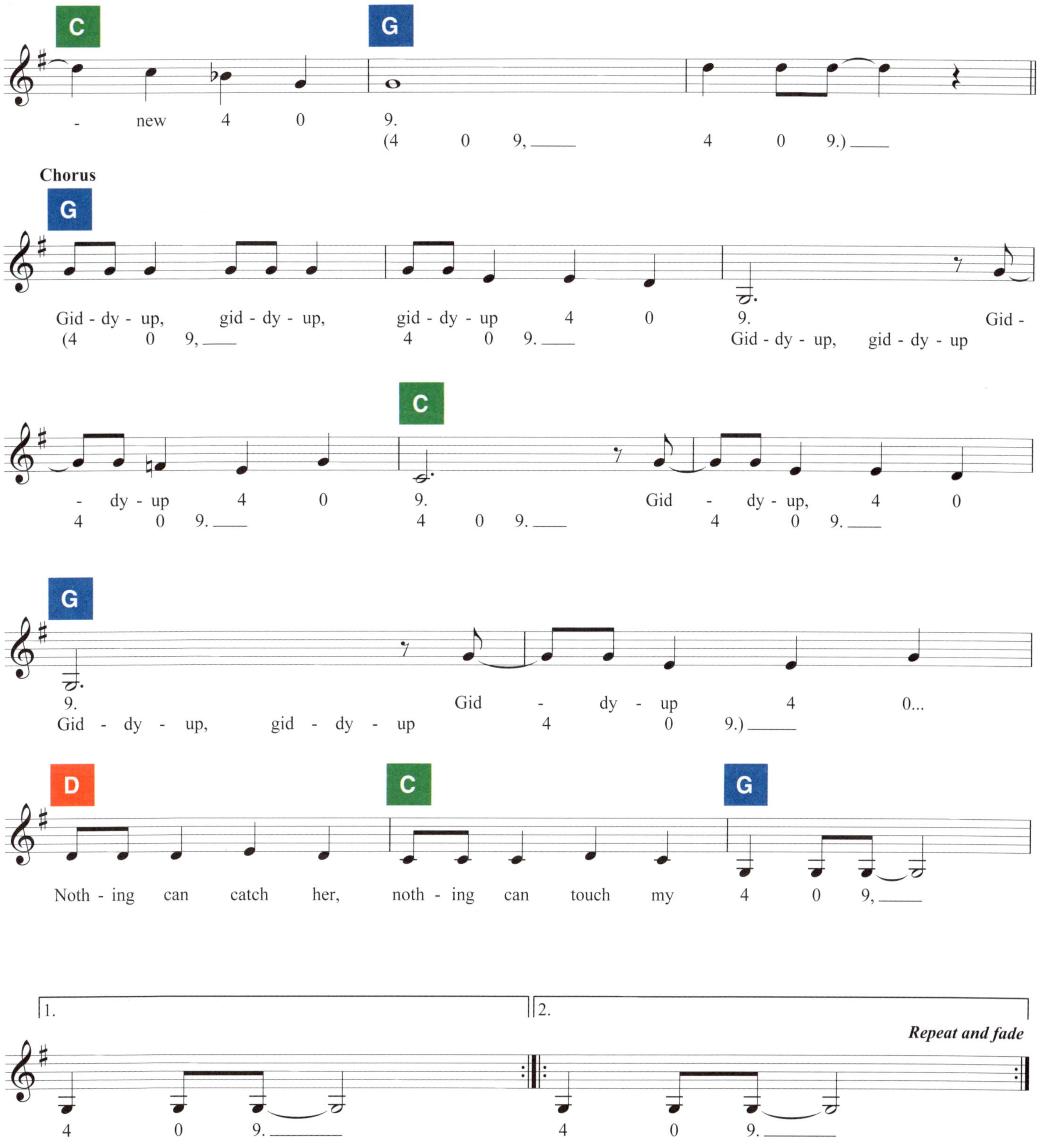

Additional Lyrics

2. When I take her to the drag, she really shines.
   (Giddy-up, giddy-up 409.)
   She always turns in the fastest time.
   (Giddy-up, giddy-up 409.)
   My four-speed, dual-quad, posi-traction 409.
   (409, 409.)

Girls Just Want to Have Fun

Words and Music by Robert Hazard

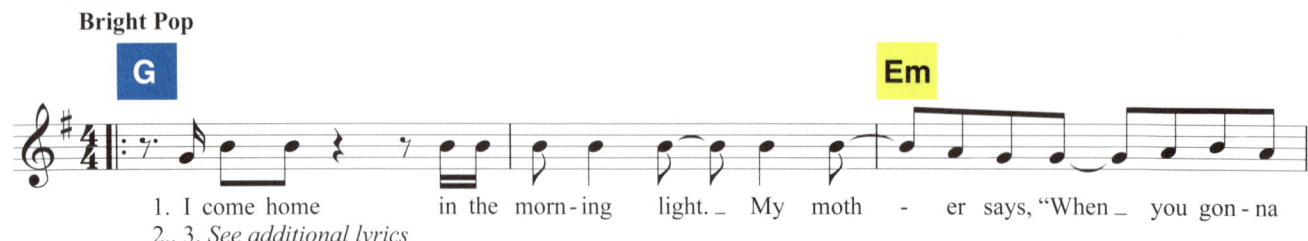

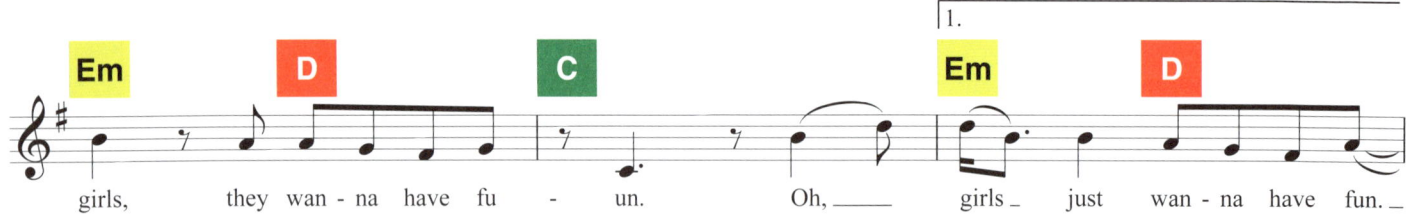

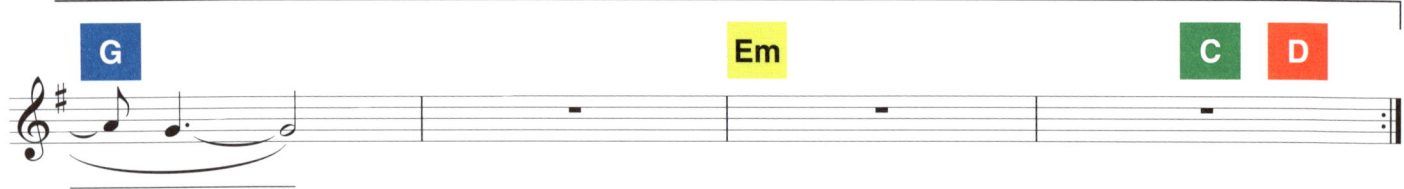

Copyright © 1979 Sony/ATV Music Publishing LLC
All Rights Administered by Sony/ATV Music Publishing LLC, 424 Church Street, Suite 1200, Nashville, TN 37219
International Copyright Secured   All Rights Reserved

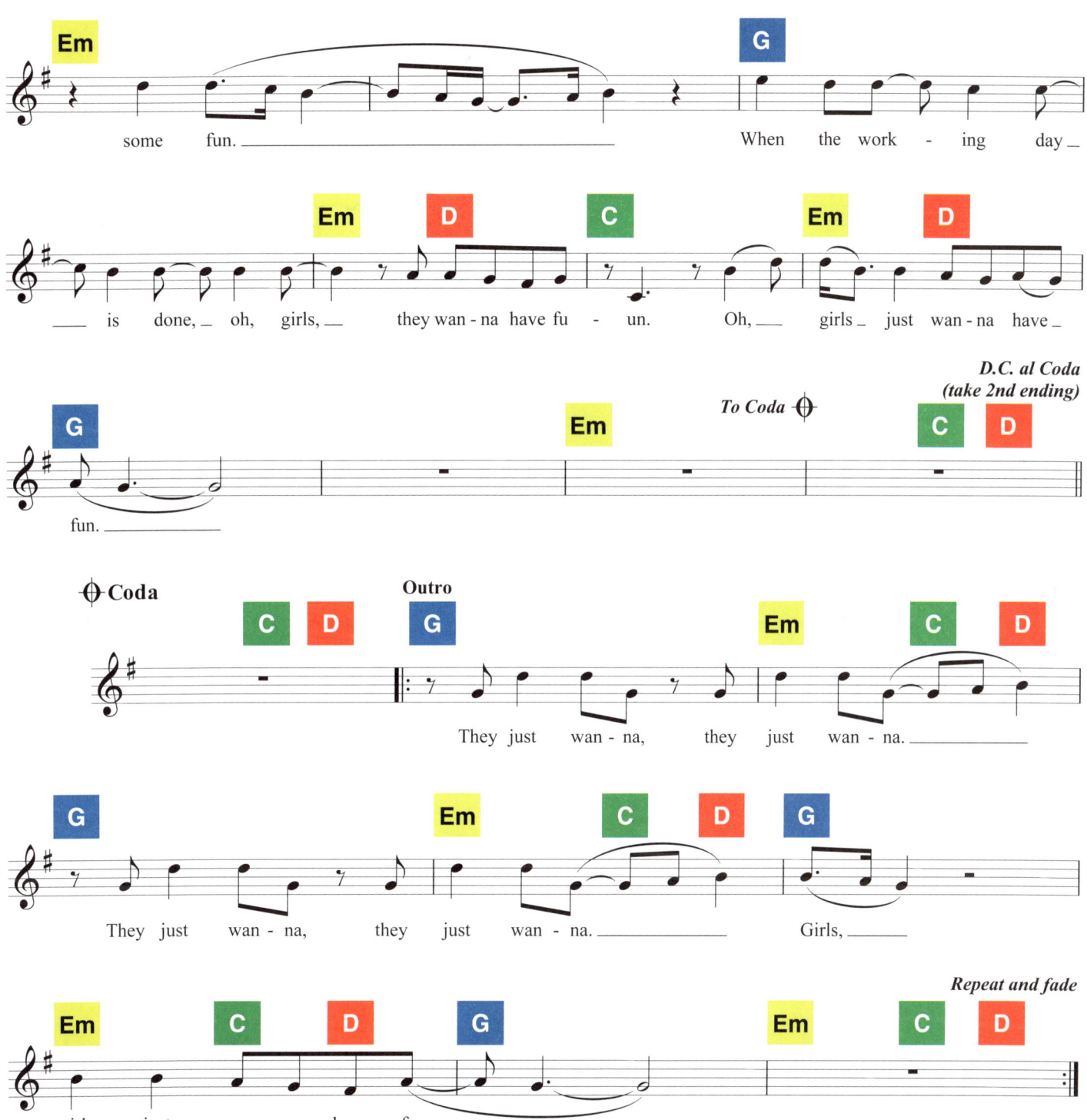

Additional Lyrics

2. The phone rings in the middle of the night.
   My father yells, "What you gonna do with your life?"
   Oh, Daddy dear, you know you're still number one.
   But girls, they wanna have fun.
   Oh, girls just wanna have... *(To Bridge)*

3. Some boys take a beautiful girl
   And hide her away from the rest of the world.
   I wanna be the one to walk in the sun.
   Oh, girls, they wanna have fun.
   Oh, girls just wanna have... *(To Bridge)*

Good Riddance
(Time of Your Life)

Words by Billie Joe
Music by Green Day

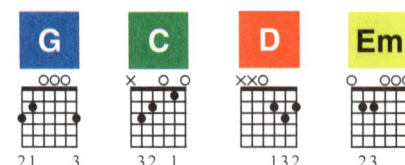

Verse
Moderately, in 2

1. An - oth - er turn - ing point, a fork
2. So take the pho - to - graphs and still -

stuck in the road. Time grabs you by
frames in your mind. Hang it on

the wrist, di - rects you where to go.
a shelf in good health and good time.

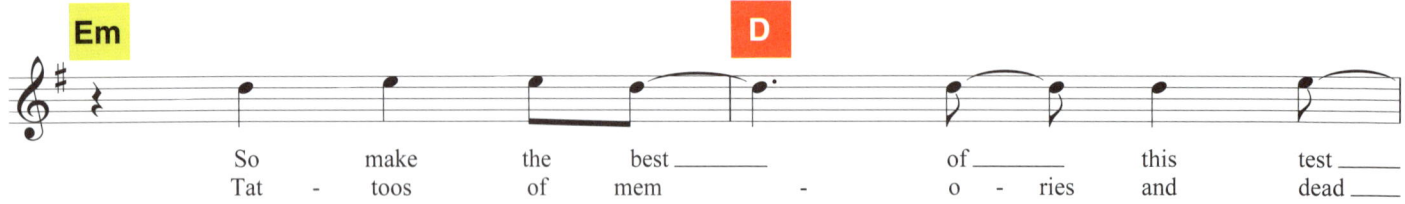

So make the best of this test
Tat - toos of mem - o - ries and dead

and don't ask why.
skin on trial.

© 1997 WB MUSIC CORP. and GREEN DAZE MUSIC
All Rights Administered by WB MUSIC CORP.
All Rights Reserved   Used by Permission

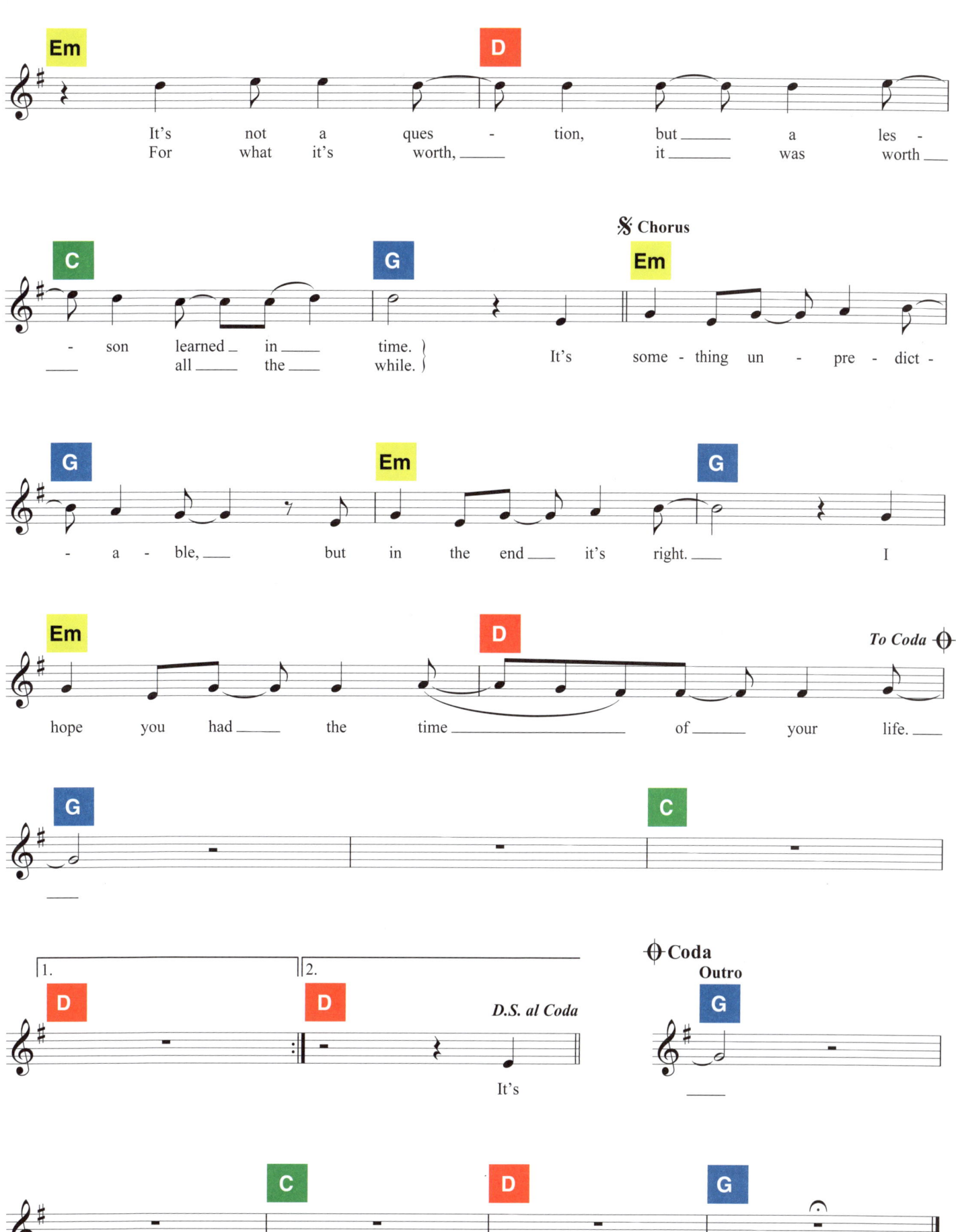

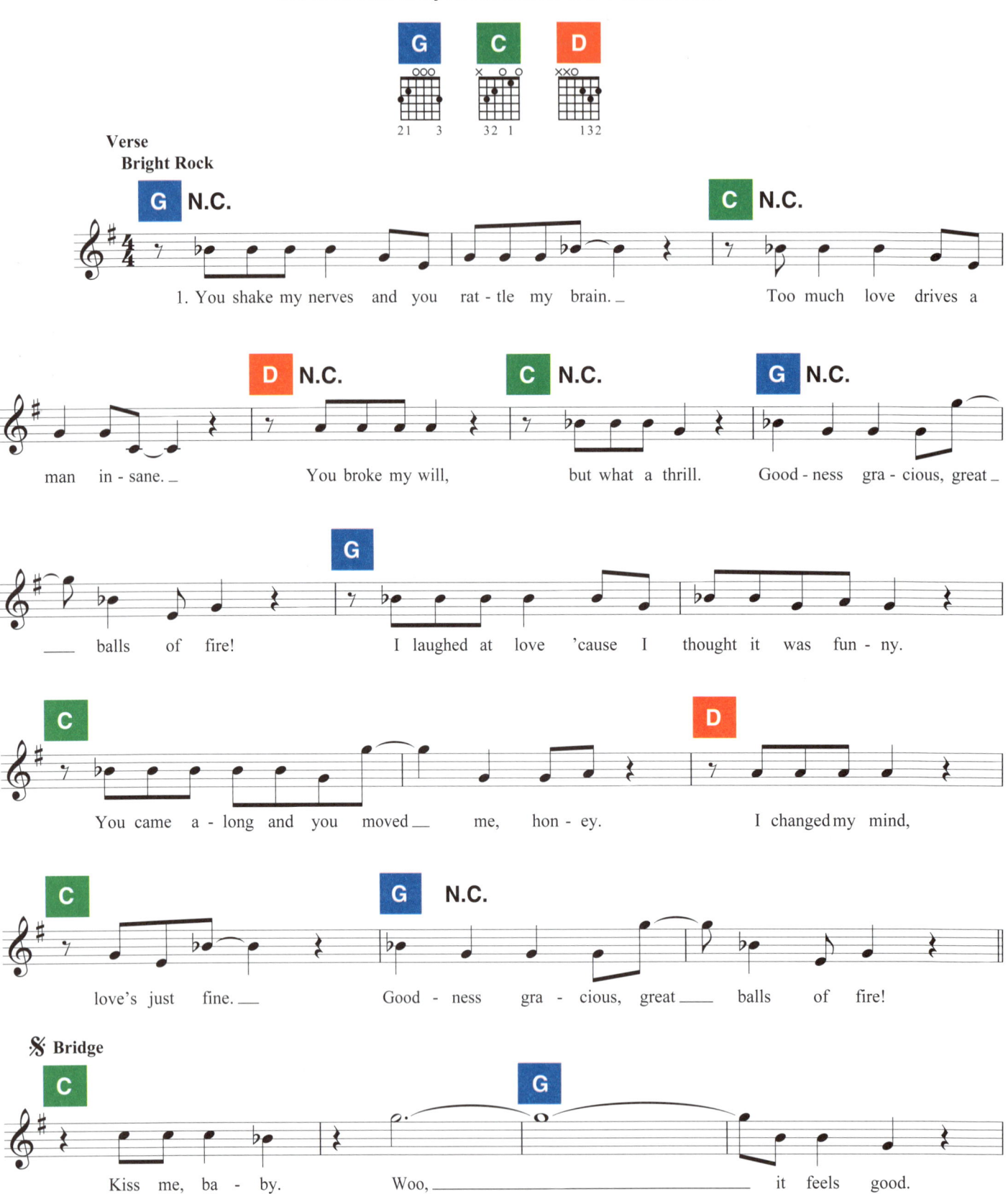

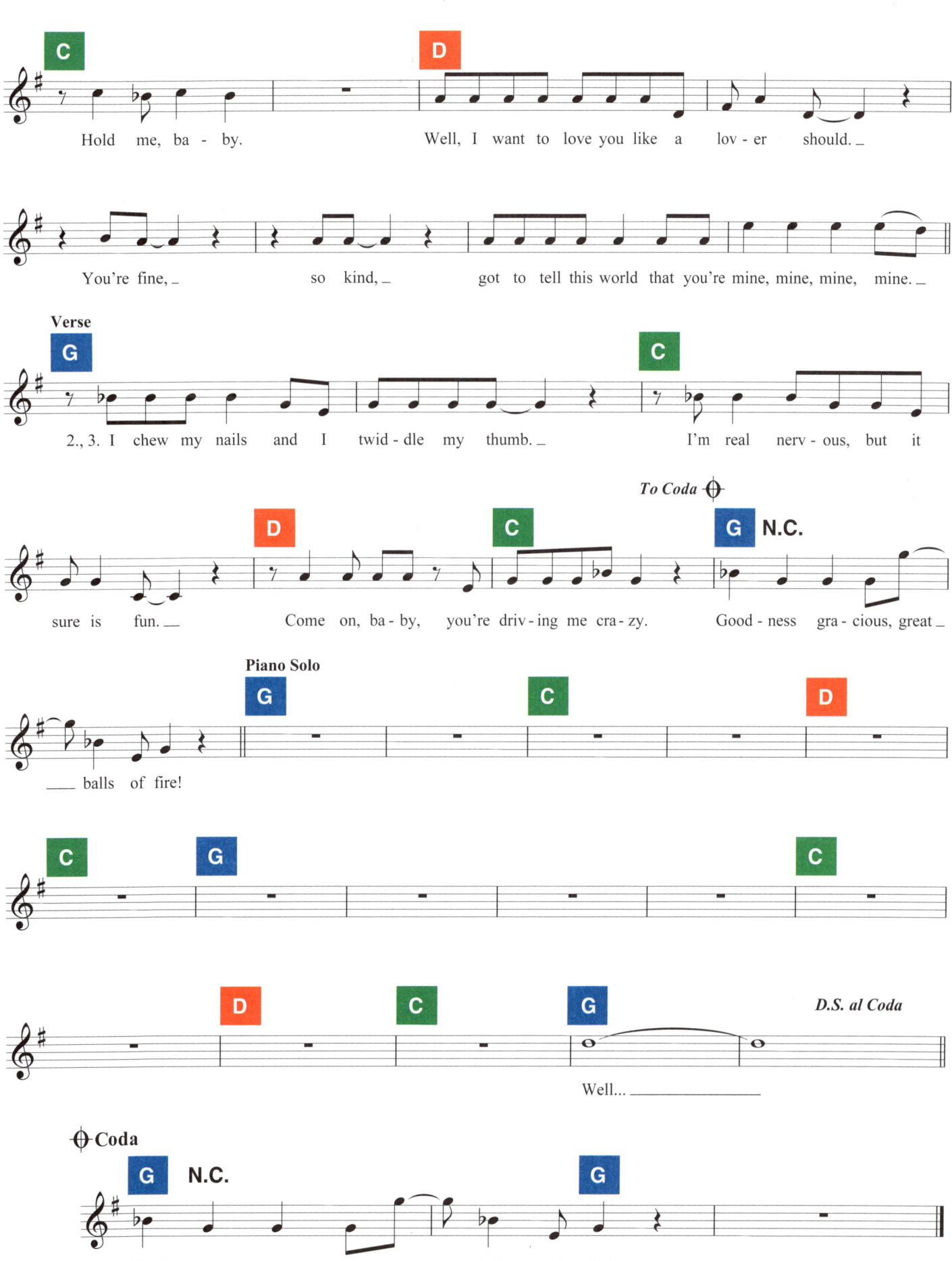

The Green Door

Words and Music by Bob Davie and Marvin Moore

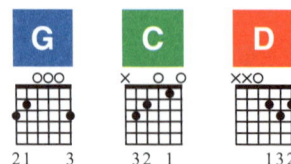

1. Mid - night;_____ one more night with - out sleep - in'._____ Watch - ing till the morn - ing comes peep - in'._____
2. Knocked once;_____ tried to tell 'em I'd been there._____ Door slammed;_____ hos - pi - tal - i - ty's thin there._____

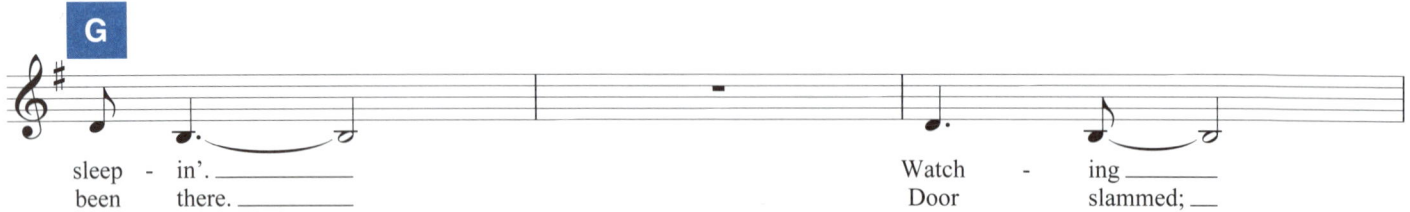

Green door,_____ what's the se - cret you're keep - in'?_____
Won - der_____ just what's go - in' on in there._____

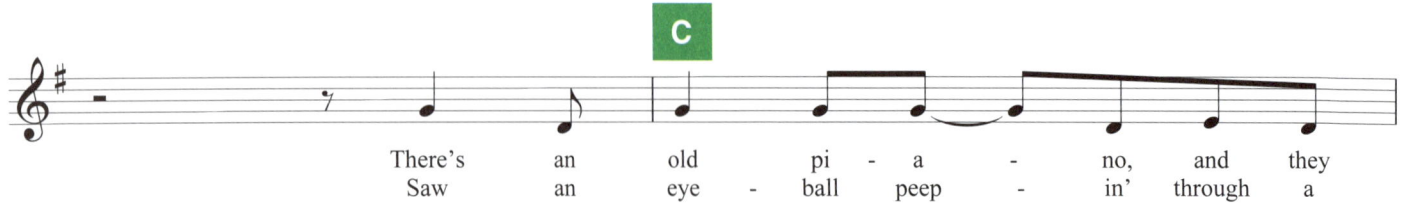

There's an old pi - a - no, and they
Saw an eye - ball peep - in' through a

Copyright © 1956 by Alley Music Corp. and Trio Music Company
Copyright Renewed
All Rights for Trio Music Company Administered by BUG Music, Inc., a BMG Chrysalis company
International Copyright Secured   All Rights Reserved
Used by Permission

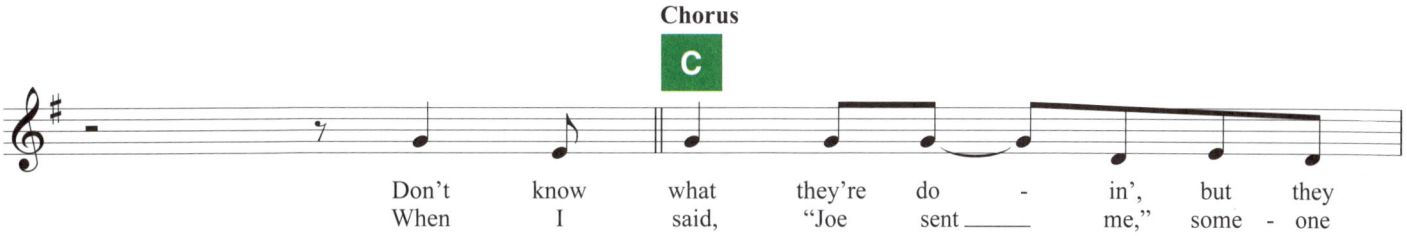
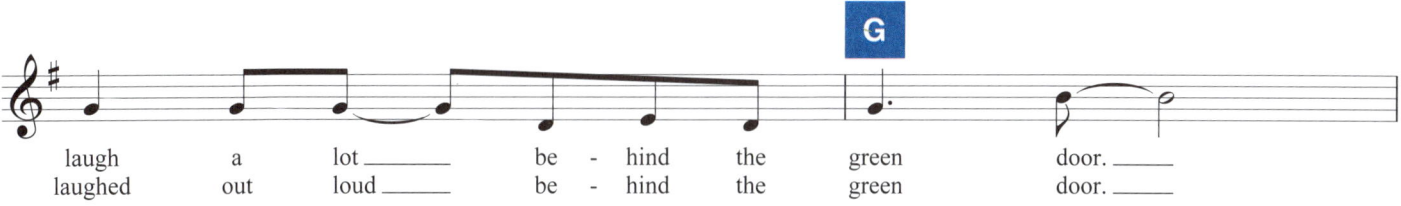

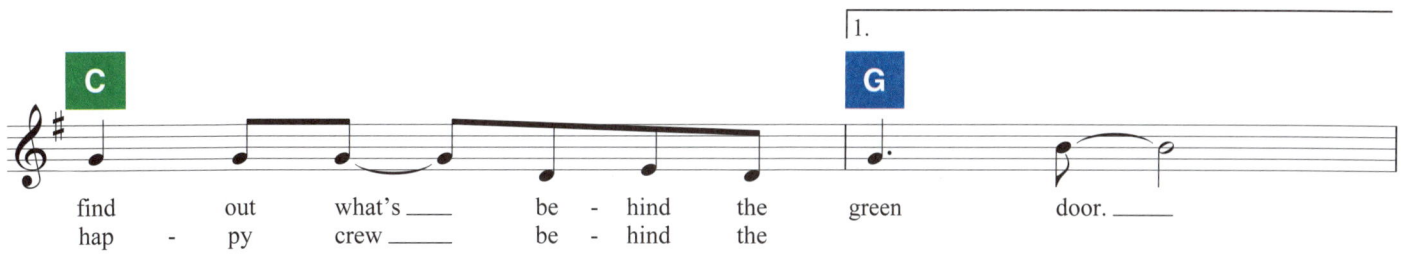

Hush-a-bye

Words by Mort Shuman
Music by Doc Pomus

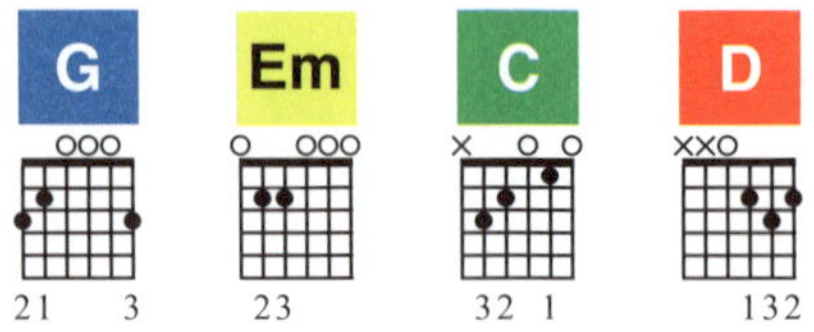

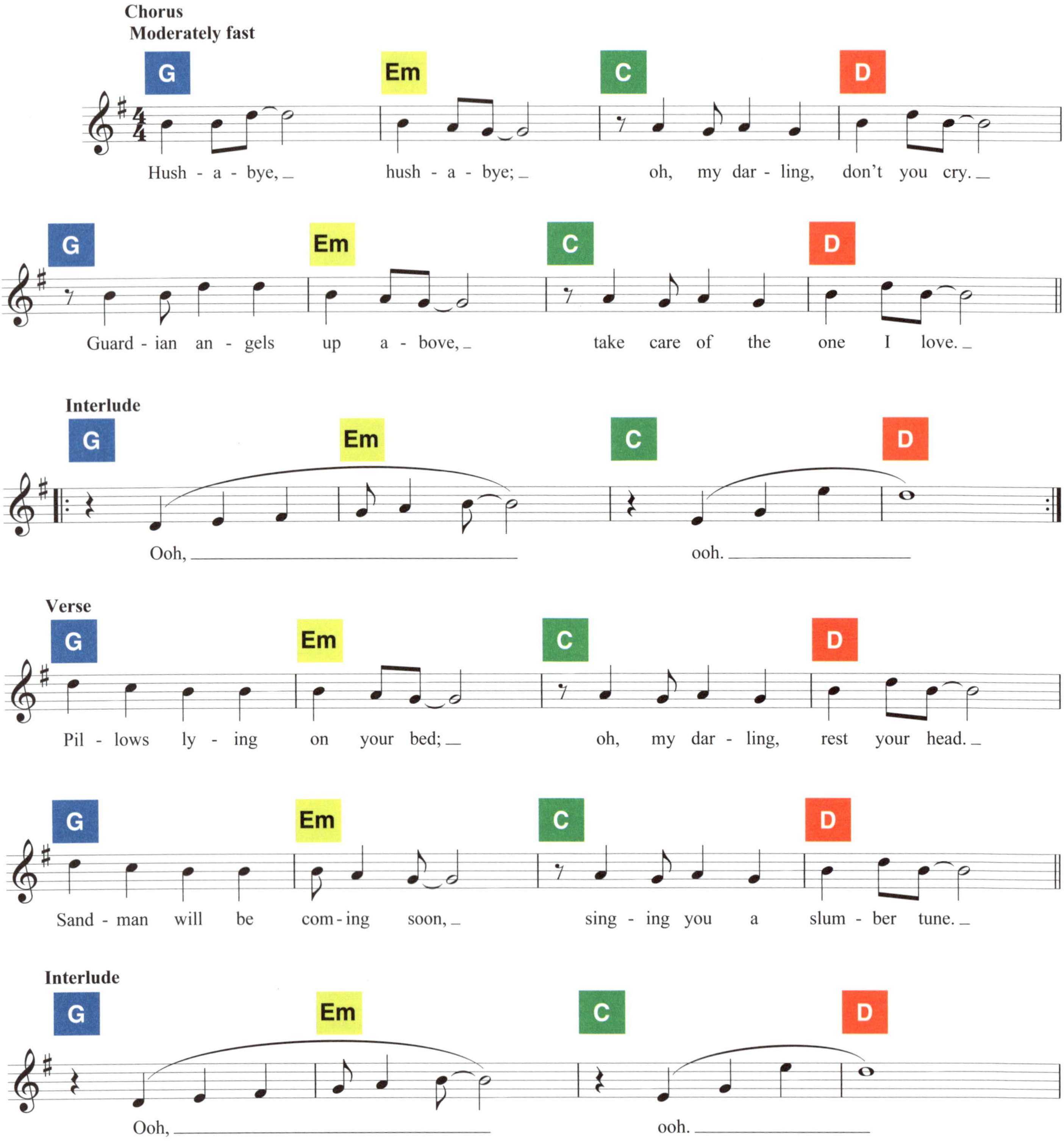

Chorus
Moderately fast

Hush - a - bye, __ hush - a - bye; __ oh, my dar - ling, don't you cry. __

Guard - ian an - gels up a - bove, __ take care of the one I love. __

Interlude

Ooh, _____ ooh. _____

Verse

Pil - lows ly - ing on your bed; __ oh, my dar - ling, rest your head. __

Sand - man will be com - ing soon, __ sing - ing you a slum - ber tune. __

Interlude

Ooh, _____ ooh. _____

© 1959 (Renewed) UNICHAPPELL MUSIC, INC.
All Rights Reserved   Used by Permission

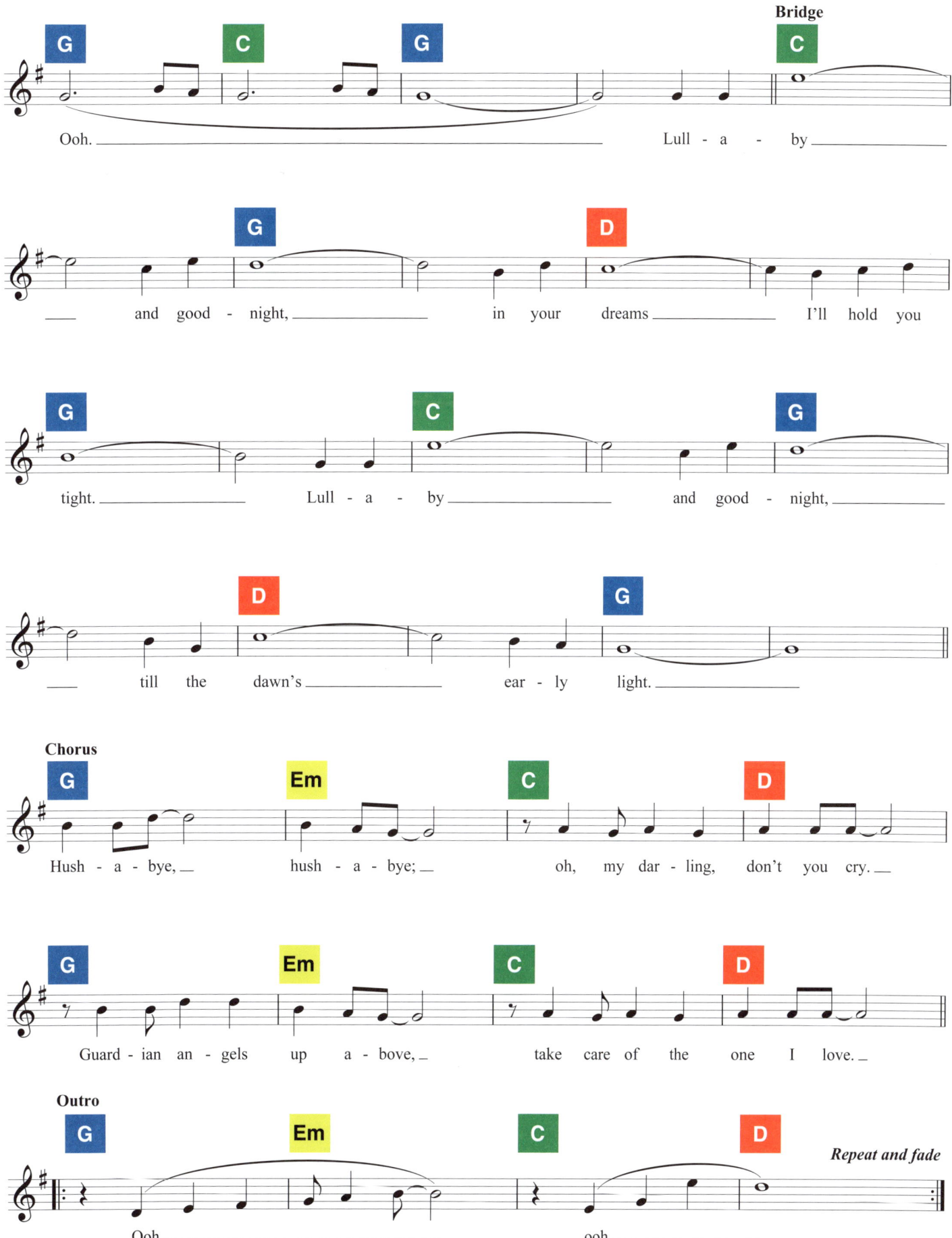

I Surrender All

Words by J.W. Van Deventer
Music by W.S. Weeden

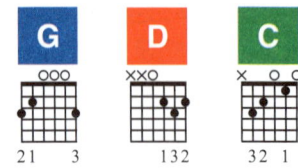

1. All to Jesus I surrender; all to Him I freely give.
2.–5. *See additional lyrics*

I will ever love and trust Him, in His presence daily live.

I surrender all, I surrender all, all to Thee, my

blessed Savior, I surrender all. all.

Additional Lyrics

2. All to Jesus I surrender; humbly at His feet I bow.
   Worldly pleasures all forsaken; take me, Jesus, take me now.

3. All to Jesus I surrender; make me, Savior, wholly Thine.
   Let me feel Thy Holy Spirit, truly know that Thou art mine.

4. All to Jesus I surrender; Lord, I give myself to Thee.
   Fill me with Thy love and power; let Thy blessing fall on me.

5. All to Jesus I surrender; now I feel the sacred flame.
   O the joy of full salvation! Glory, glory to His name!

Copyright © 2012 by HAL LEONARD CORPORATION
International Copyright Secured All Rights Reserved

I've Got Peace Like a River

Traditional

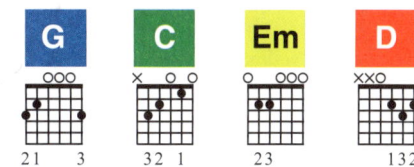

Verse
Moderately, in 2

1. I've got peace like a riv-er. I've got peace like a
2. I've got love like an o-cean. I've got love like an
3. I've got joy like a foun-tain. I've got joy like a

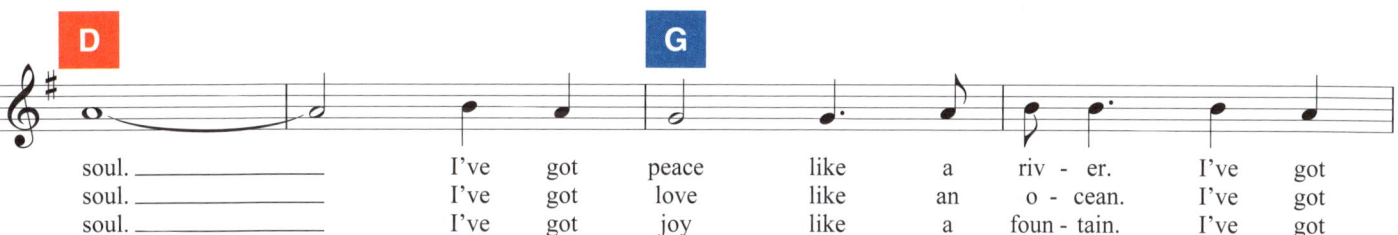

riv-er. I've got peace like a riv-er in my
o-cean. I've got love like an o-cean in my
foun-tain. I've got joy like a foun-tain in my

soul._____ I've got peace like a riv-er. I've got
soul._____ I've got love like an o-cean. I've got
soul._____ I've got joy like a foun-tain. I've got

peace like a riv-er. I've got peace like a
love like an o-cean. I've got love like an
joy like a foun-tain. I've got joy like a

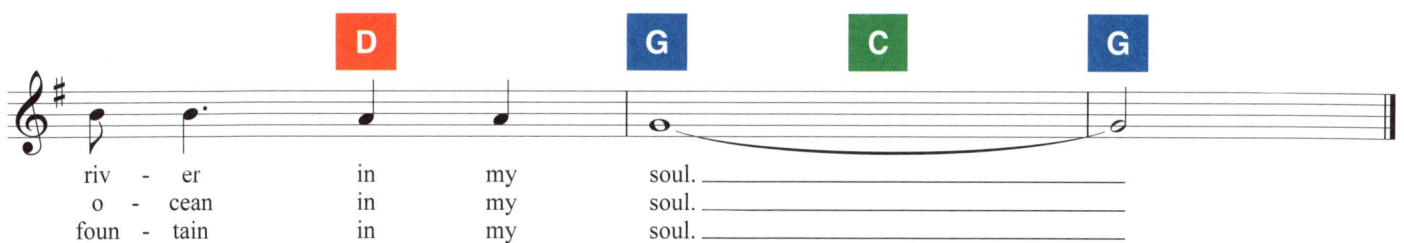

riv-er in my soul._____
o-cean in my soul._____
foun-tain in my soul._____

Copyright © 2015 by HAL LEONARD CORPORATION
International Copyright Secured All Rights Reserved

It's Hard to Be Humble

Words and Music by Mac Davis

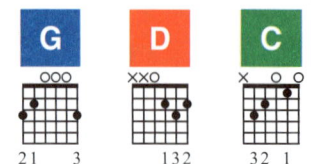

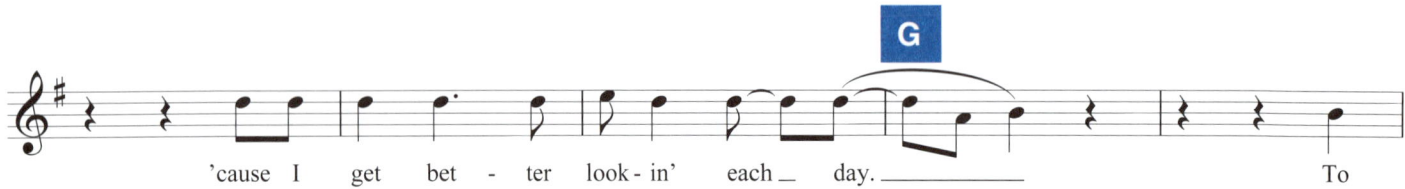

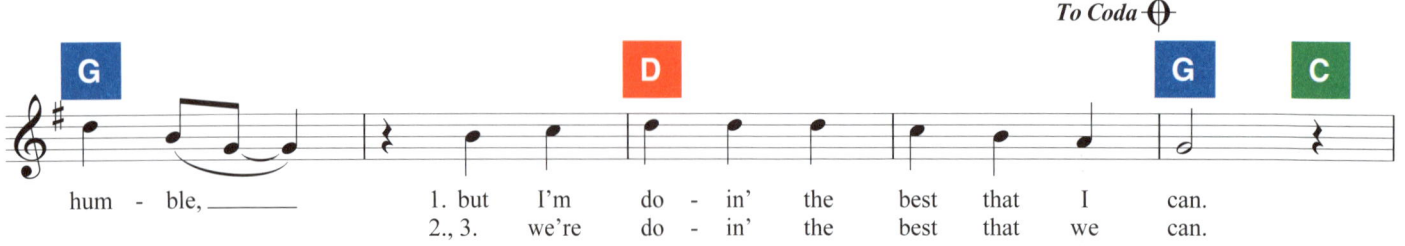

Copyright © 1980 Primary Wave Brian and Songpainter Music
All Rights Administered BMG Rights Management (US) LLC
All Rights Reserved   Used by Permission

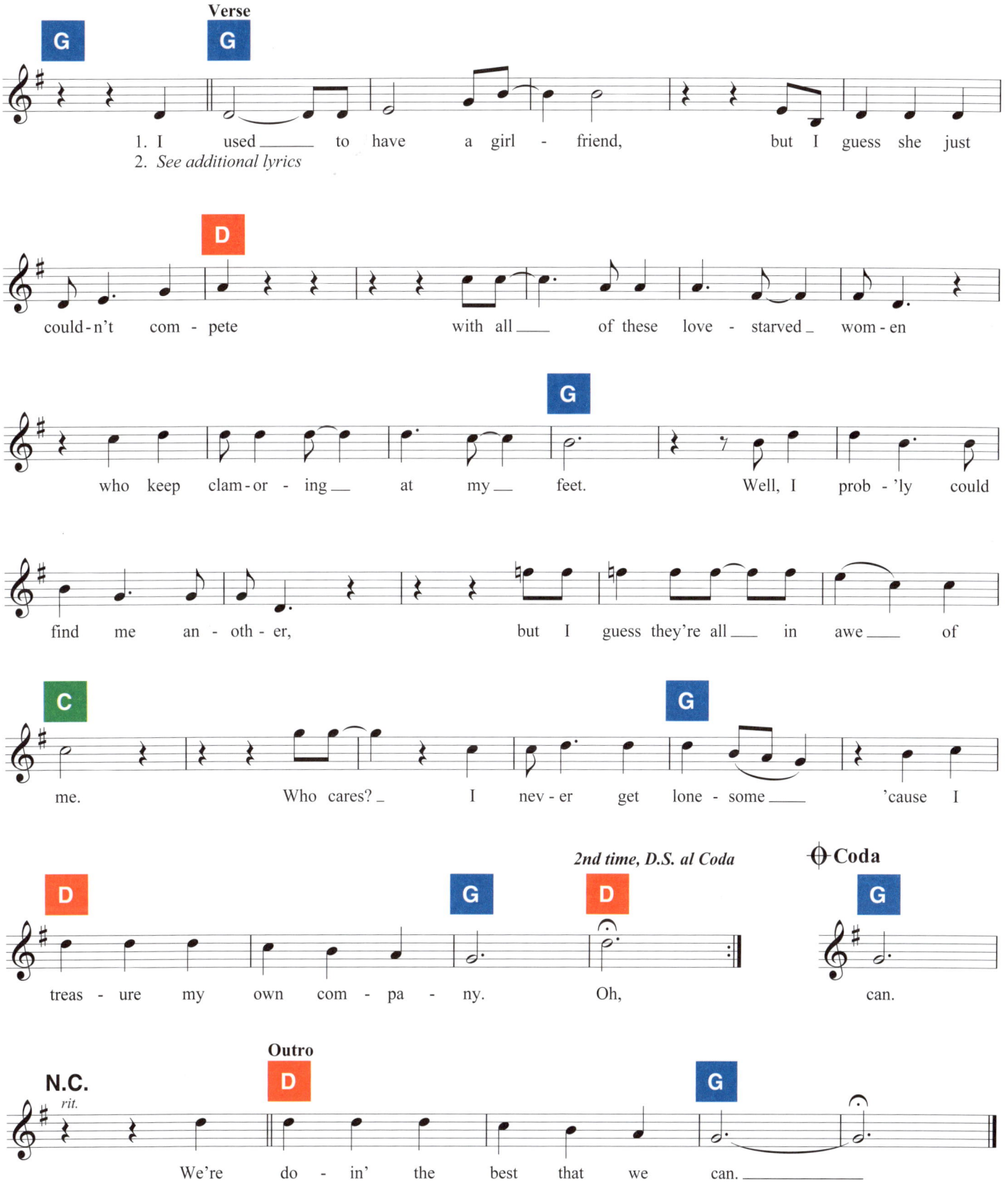

Additional Lyrics

2. I guess you could say I'm a loner, a cowboy outlaw, tough and proud.
   Oh, I could have lots of friends if I wanna, but then I wouldn't stand out from the crowd.
   Some folks say that I'm egotistical. Hell, I don't even know what that means.
   I guess it has something to do with the way that I fill out my skin-tight blue jeans.

Leaning on the Everlasting Arms

Words by Elisha A. Hoffman
Music by Anthony J. Showalter

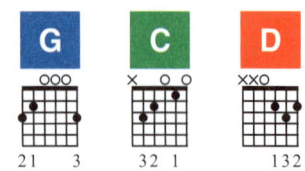

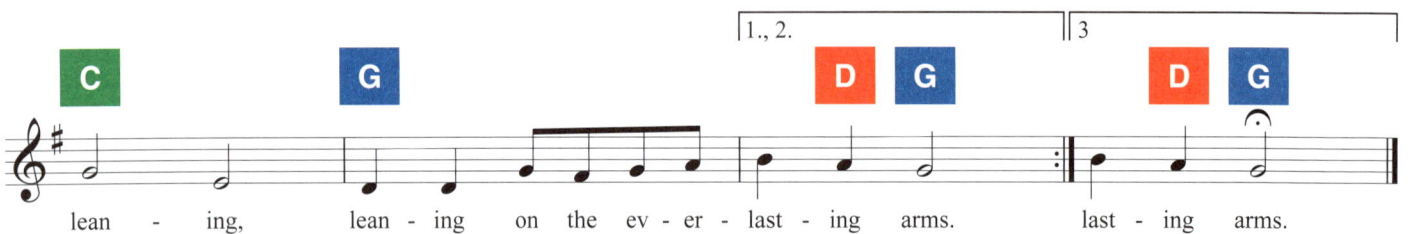

Additional Lyrics

2. Oh, how sweet to walk in this pilgrim way,
   Leaning on the everlasting arms.
   Oh, how bright the path grows from day to day,
   Leaning on the everlasting arms.

3. What have I to dread, what have I to fear,
   Leaning on the everlasting arms?
   I have blessed peace with my Lord so near,
   Leaning on the everlasting arms.

Copyright © 2012 by HAL LEONARD CORPORATION
International Copyright Secured   All Rights Reserved

Nearer, My God, to Thee

Words by Sarah F. Adams
Based on Genesis 28:10-22
Music by Lowell Mason

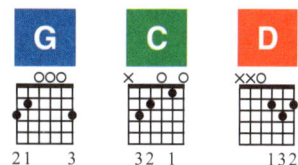

1. Near-er, my God, to Thee, near-er to Thee,
2.–4. *See additional lyrics*

E'en though it be a cross that raise-eth me.

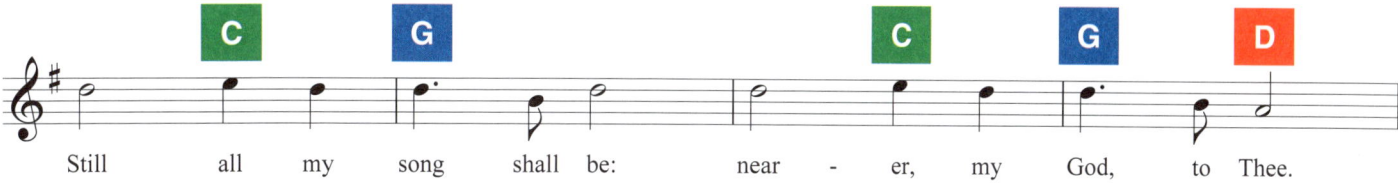

Still all my song shall be: near-er, my God, to Thee.

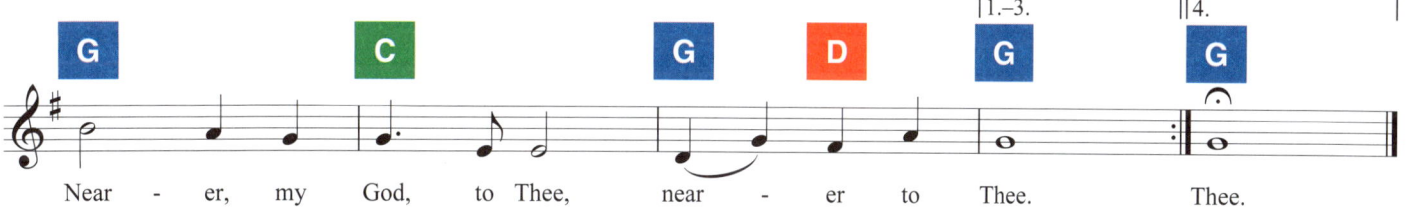

Near-er, my God, to Thee, near-er to Thee. Thee.

Additional Lyrics

2. Though, like the wanderer, the sun go down,
   Darkness be over me, my rest a stone;
   Yet in my dreams I'd be nearer, my God, to Thee.
   Nearer, my God, to Thee, nearer to Thee.

3. Then with my waking thoughts bright with Thy praise,
   Out of my stony griefs Bethel I'll raise;
   So by my woes to be nearer, my God, to Thee.
   Nearer, my God, to Thee, nearer to Thee.

4. Or if on joyful wing, cleaving the sky,
   Sun, moon and stars forgot, upward I fly;
   Still all my song shall be: nearer, my God, to Thee.
   Nearer, my God, to Thee, nearer to Thee.

Copyright © 2012 by HAL LEONARD CORPORATION
International Copyright Secured   All Rights Reserved

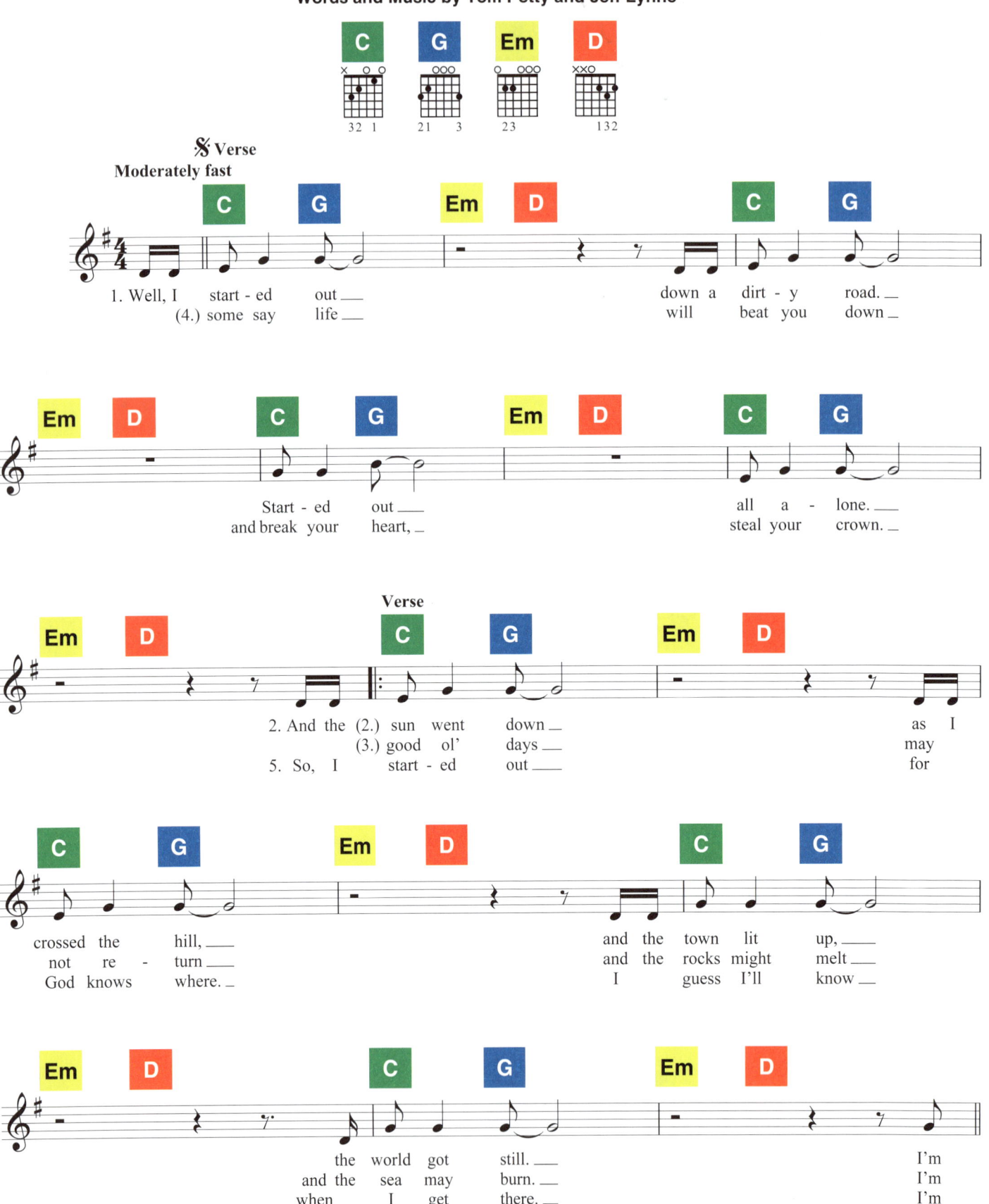

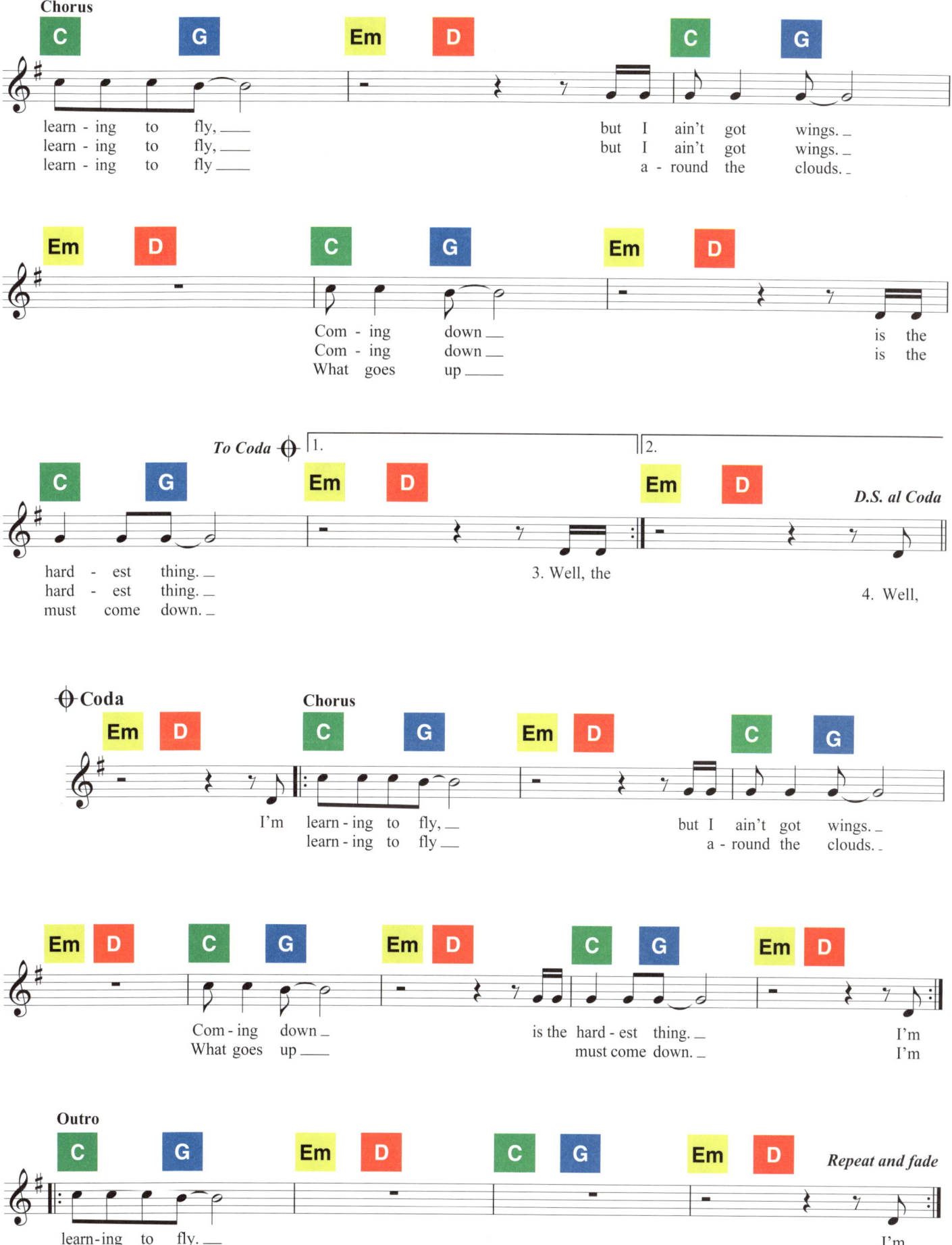

Lookin' Out My Back Door

Words and Music by John Fogerty

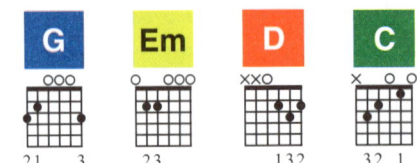

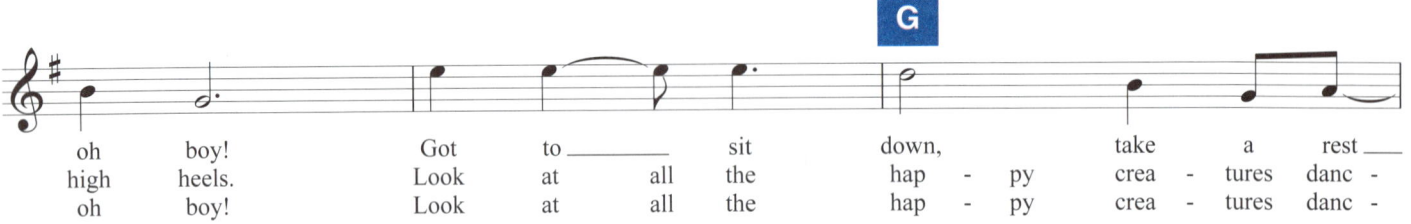

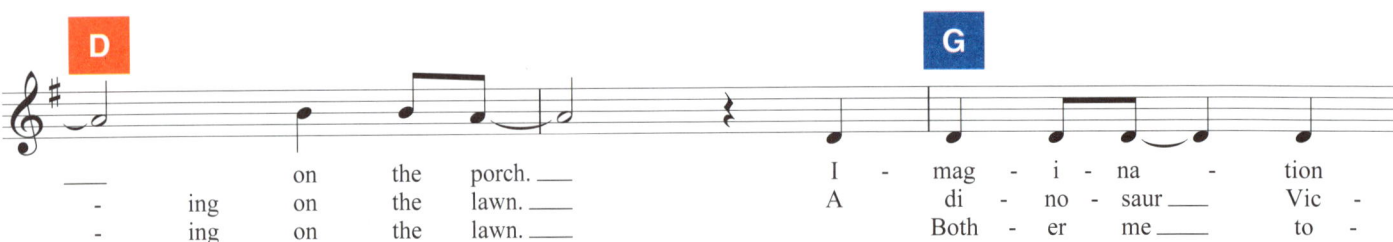

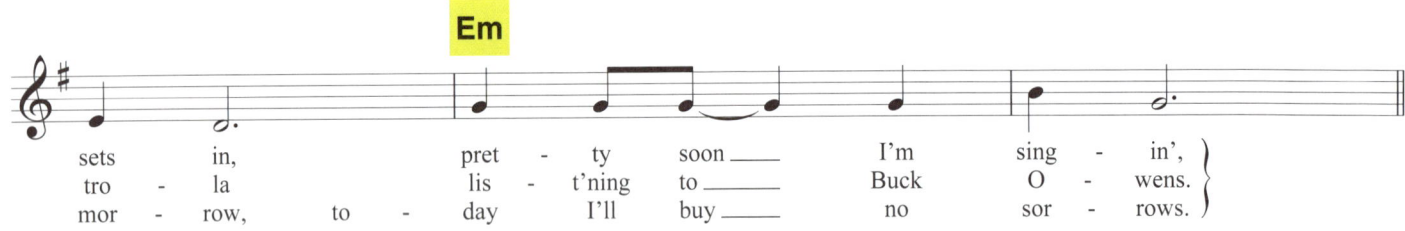

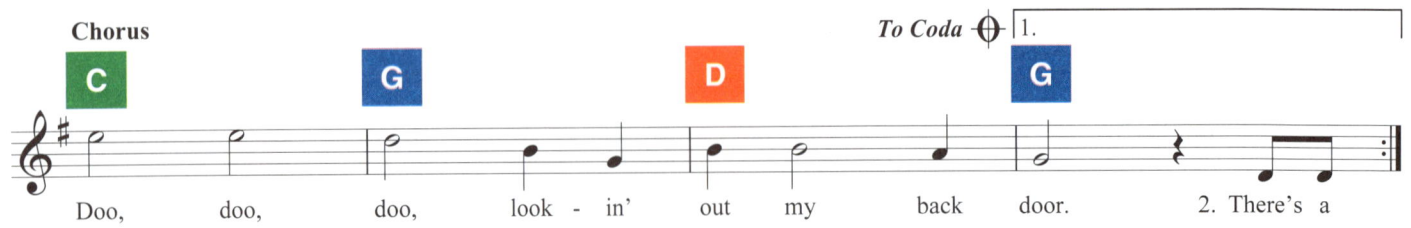

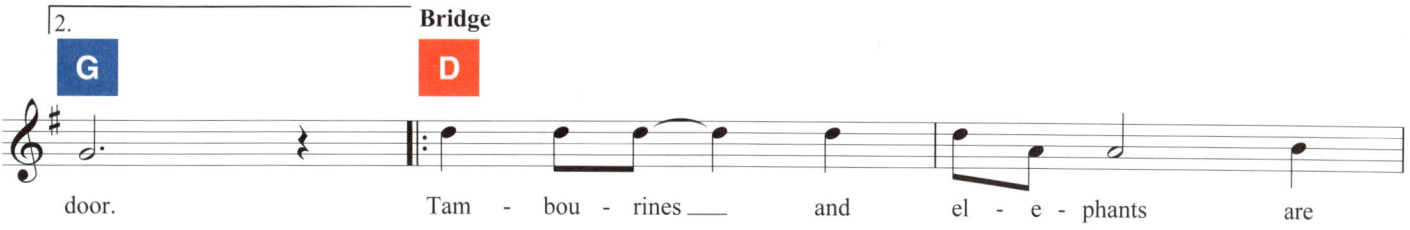
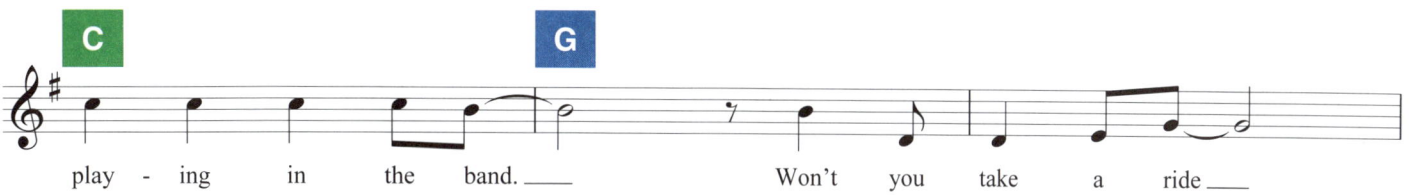
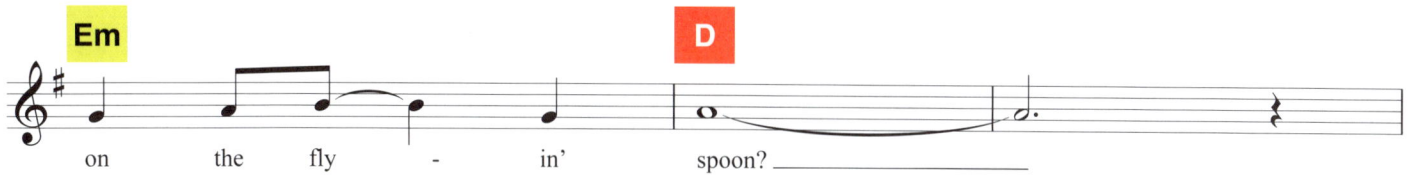
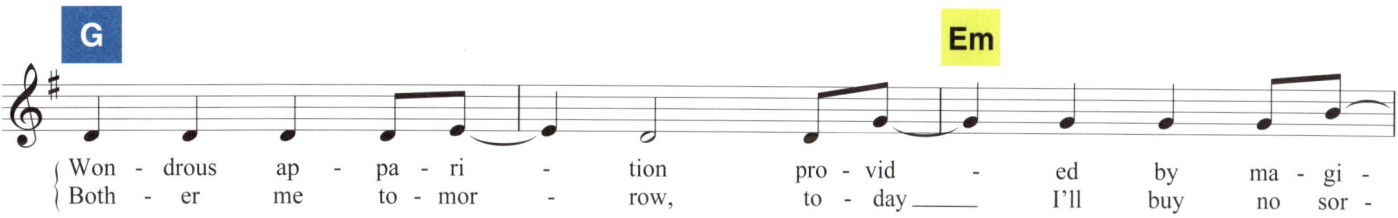
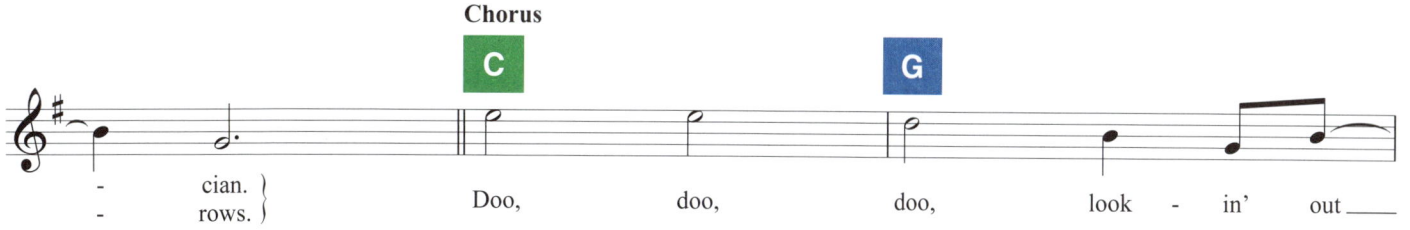

The Old Rugged Cross

Words and Music by Rev. George Bennard

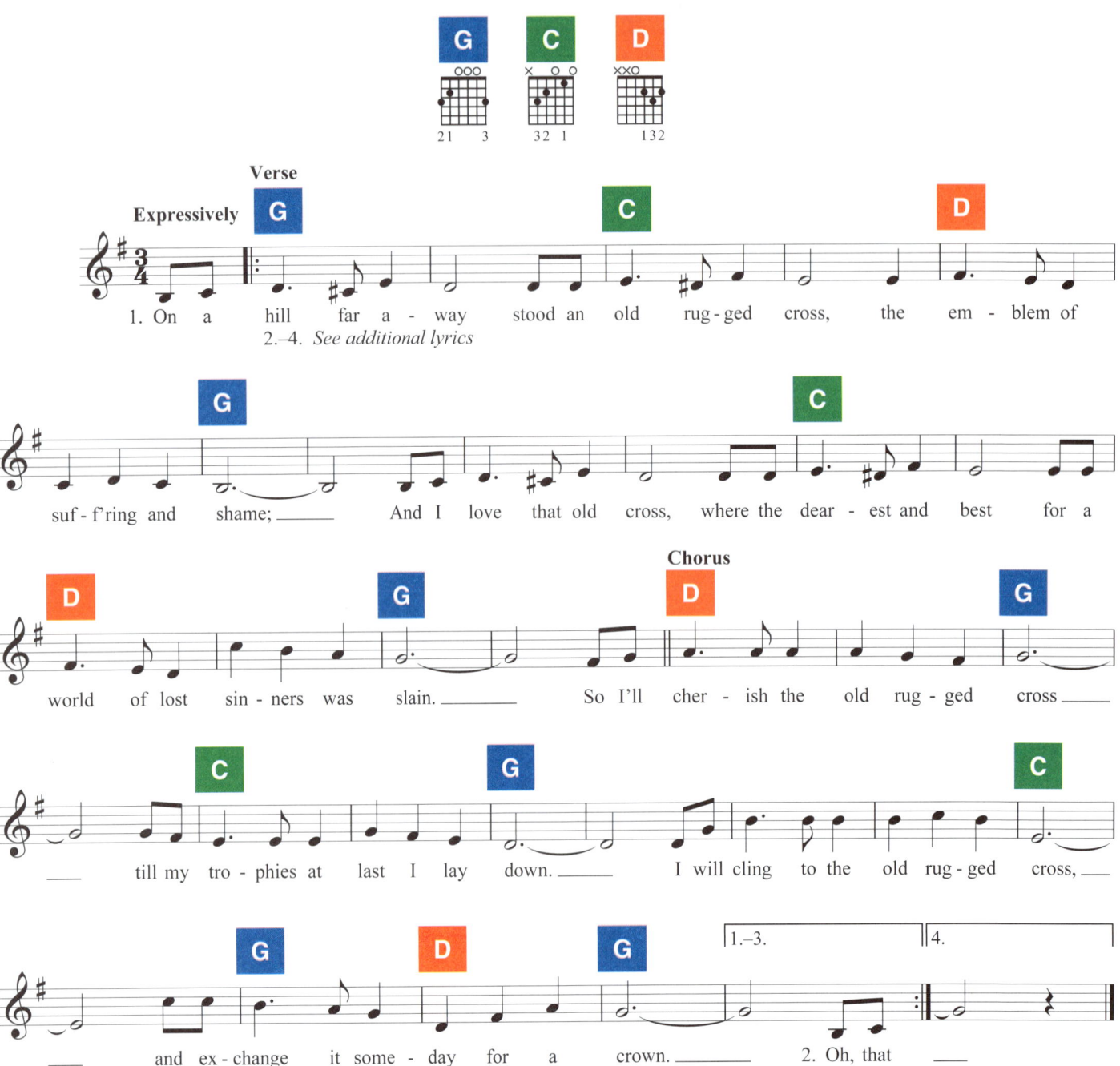

Additional Lyrics

2. Oh, that old rugged cross, so despised by the world,
   Has a wondrous attraction for me;
   For the dear Lamb of God left His glory above
   To bear it to dark Calvary.

3. In the old rugged cross, stained with blood so divine,
   Such a wonderful beauty I see;
   For 'twas on that old cross Jesus suffered and died
   To pardon and sanctify me.

4. To the old rugged cross I will ever be true,
   Its shame and reproach gladly bear;
   Then He'll call me someday to my home far away,
   Where His glory forever I'll share.

Copyright © 2012 by HAL LEONARD CORPORATION
International Copyright Secured   All Rights Reserved

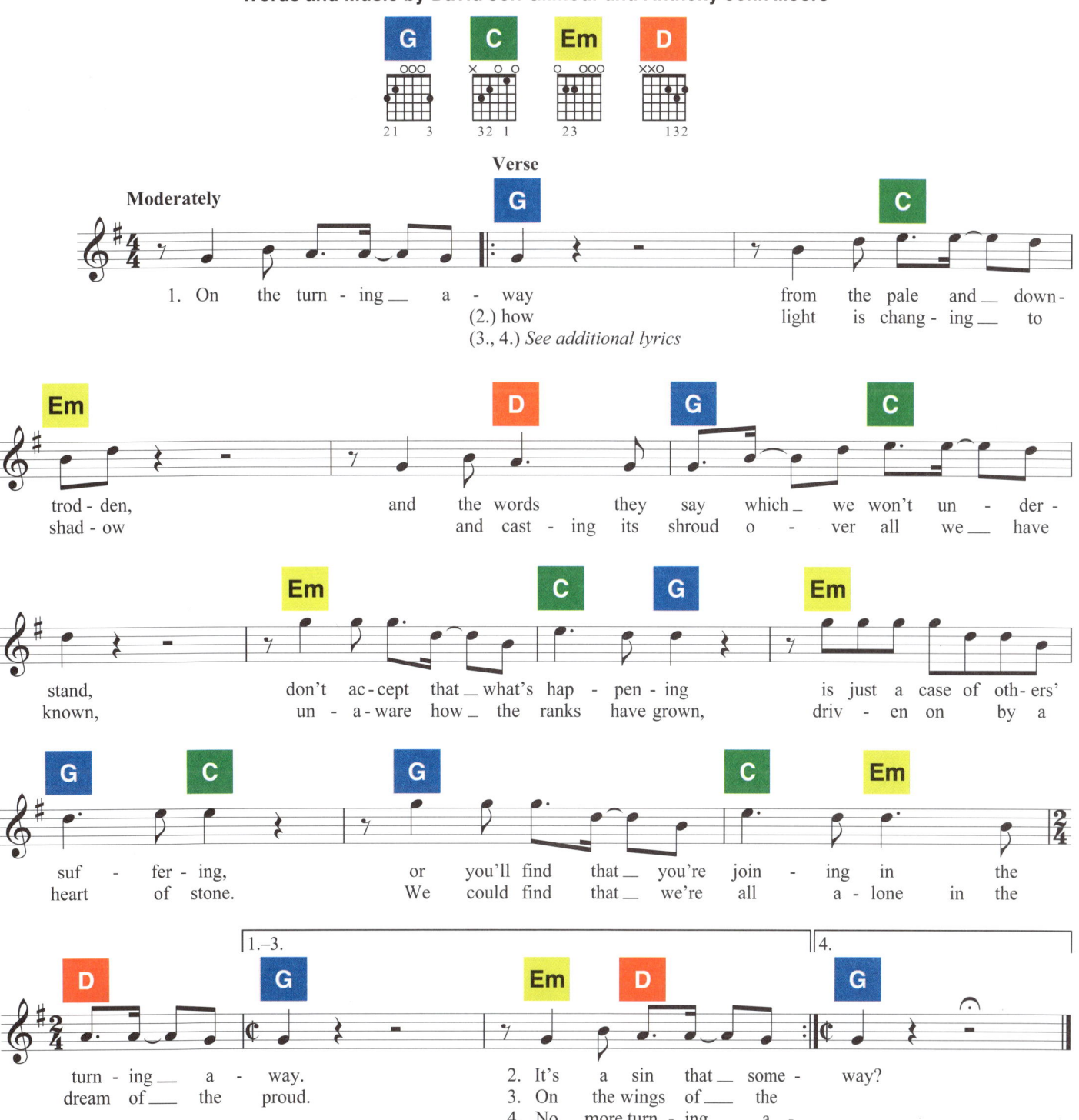

One Love
Words and Music by Bob Marley

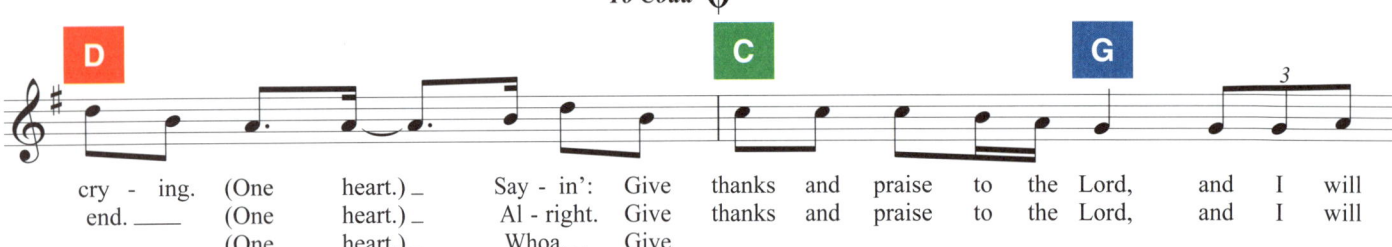

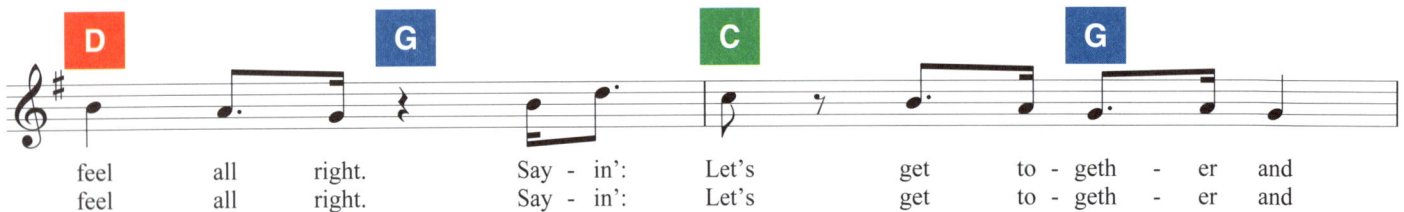

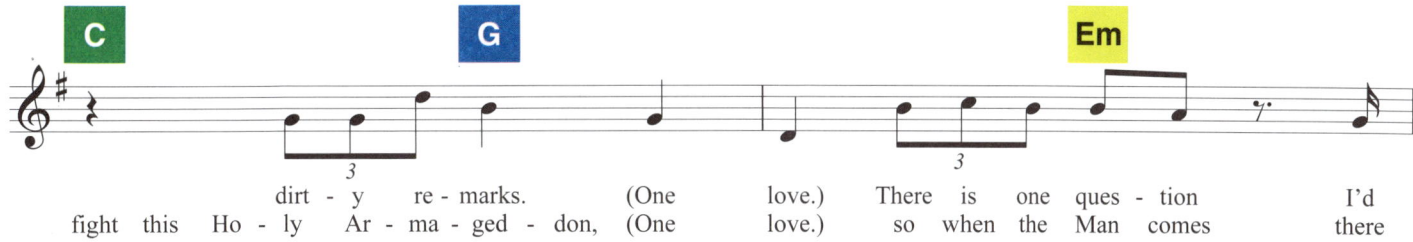
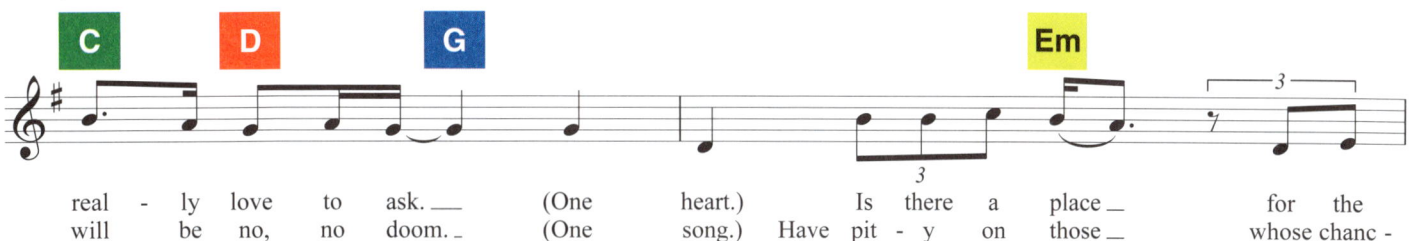

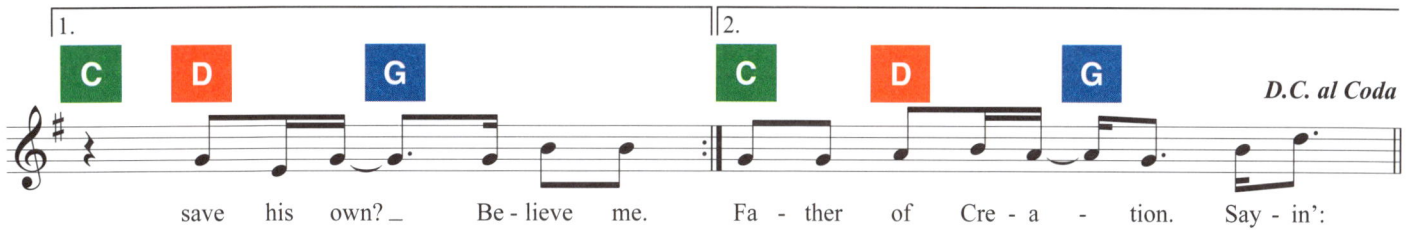

Party Doll

Words and Music by James Bowen and Buddy Knox

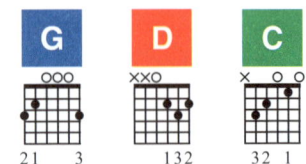

Verse
Moderately, in 2

1. All I want is a par-ty doll to come a-long with me when I'm
(2.) I saw a gal walk-in' down the street, the kind of a gal I would

feel-in' wild, to be ev-er lov-in' and
love to meet. She had blonde hair and

true and fair, to run her fin-gers a-through my hair.
eyes of blue. Ba-by, I'm a-gon-na have a par-ty with you.

𝄋 Chorus

Come a-long and be my par-ty doll. Come a-long and be my

par-ty doll. Come a-long and be my par-ty doll.

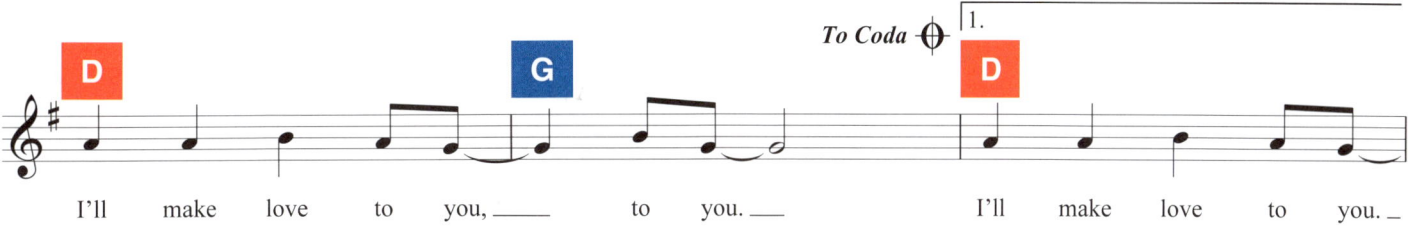

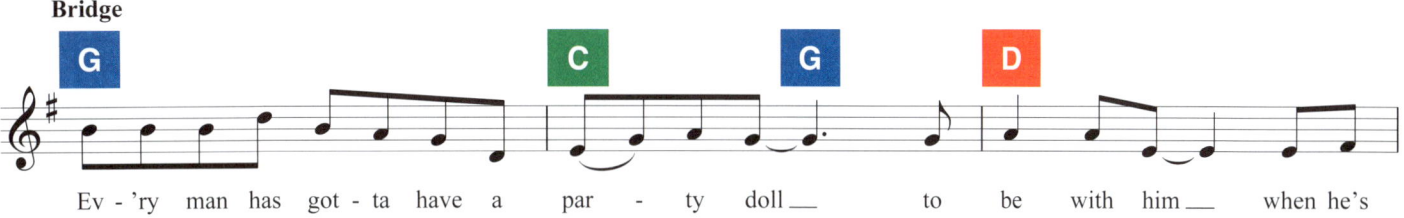

Rock Around the Clock
Words and Music by Max C. Freedman and Jimmy DeKnight

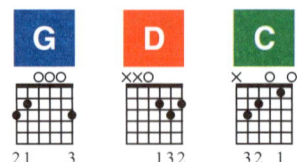

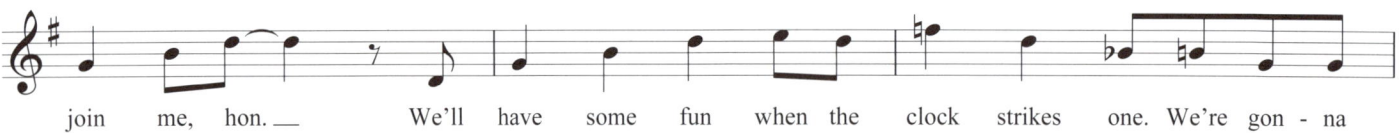

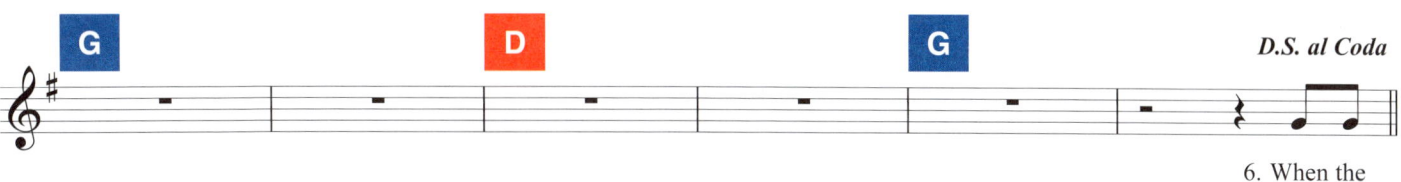
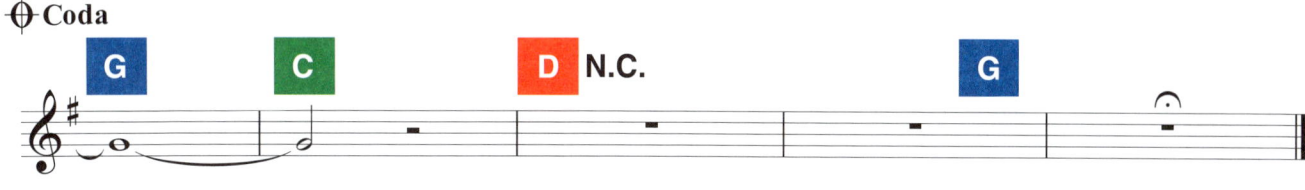

Additional Lyrics

2. When the clock strikes two, three and four,
   If the band slows down we'll yell for more.
   We're gonna rock around the clock tonight.
   We're gonna rock, rock, rock till broad daylight.
   We're gonna rock, gonna rock around the clock tonight.

4. When the chimes ring five, six and seven,
   We'll be right in seventh heaven.
   We're gonna rock around the clock tonight.
   We're gonna rock, rock, rock till broad daylight.
   We're gonna rock, gonna rock around the clock tonight.

5. When it's eight, nine, ten, eleven too,
   I'll be goin' strong and so will you.
   We're gonna rock around the clock tonight.
   We're gonna rock, rock, rock till broad daylight.
   We're gonna rock, gonna rock around the clock tonight.

6. When the clock strikes twelve, we'll cool off then,
   Start a-rockin' 'round the clock again.
   We're gonna rock around the clock tonight.
   We're gonna rock, rock, rock till broad daylight.
   We're gonna rock, gonna rock around the clock tonight.

Rock Me

Words and Music by John Kay

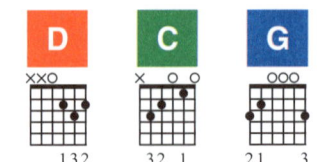

1. She asked me may-be I could share her sor-row
2. Ev-'ry-bod-y's ills, you know, it fills her with com-pas-sion.

a-bout the men that tried to treat her wrong._ 'Tho just a ba-by a-
That's why she tries to save the world a-lone._ She helps the need-y

wait-ing her to-mor-row, it's rock me, ba-by, rock me, ba-by, all night long._
in her own fash-ion and tries to give them all her own._

Pre-Chorus

She needs an an-swer to her con-fu-sion, some-one to guide her with

ten-der-ness. But if she's ask-in' for a so-lu-tion,

Copyright © 1968, 1969 SONGS OF UNIVERSAL, INC.
Copyright Renewed
All Rights Reserved   Used by Permission

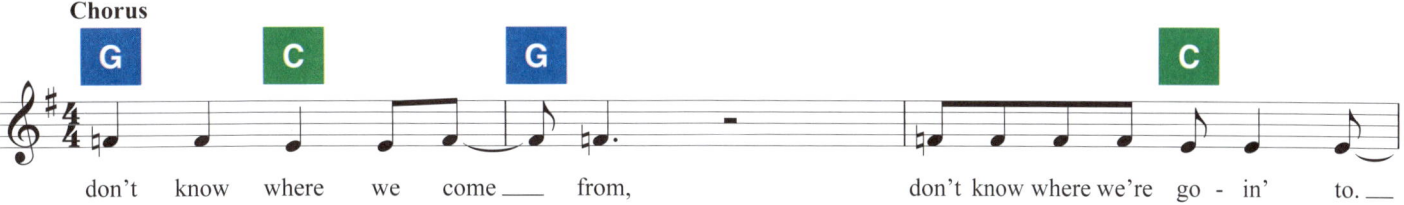

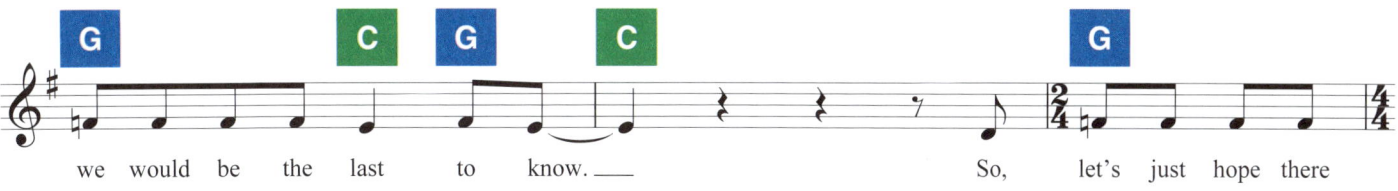

Rockin' Robin

Words and Music by J. Thomas

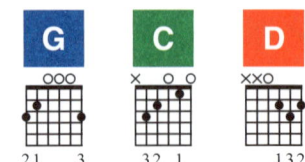

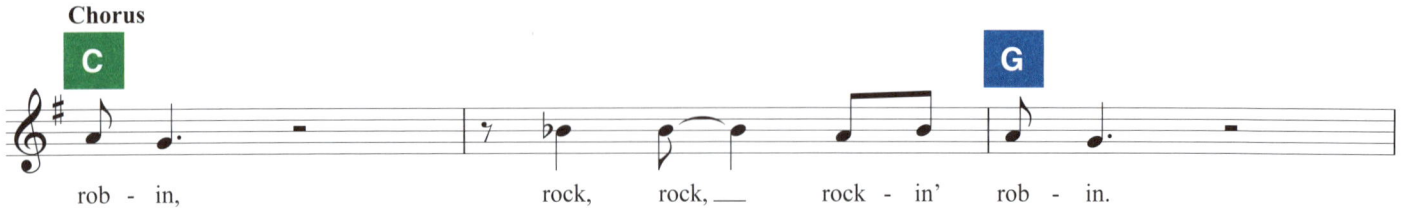

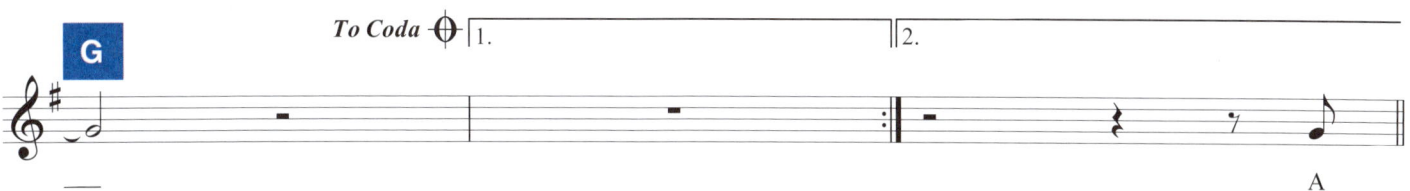
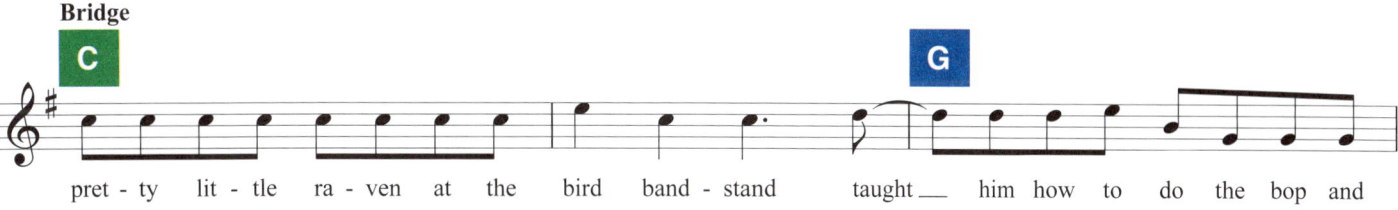

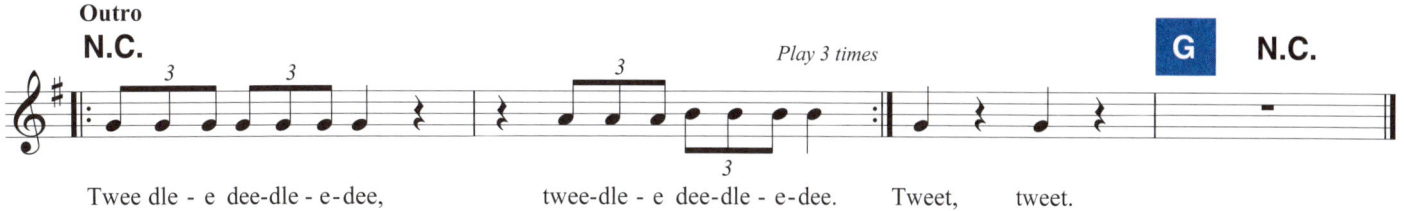

Additional Lyrics

2. Ev'ry little swallow, ev'ry chickadee,
   Ev'ry little bird in the tall oak tree,
   The wise old owl, the big black crow,
   Flap their wings singin' go, bird, go.

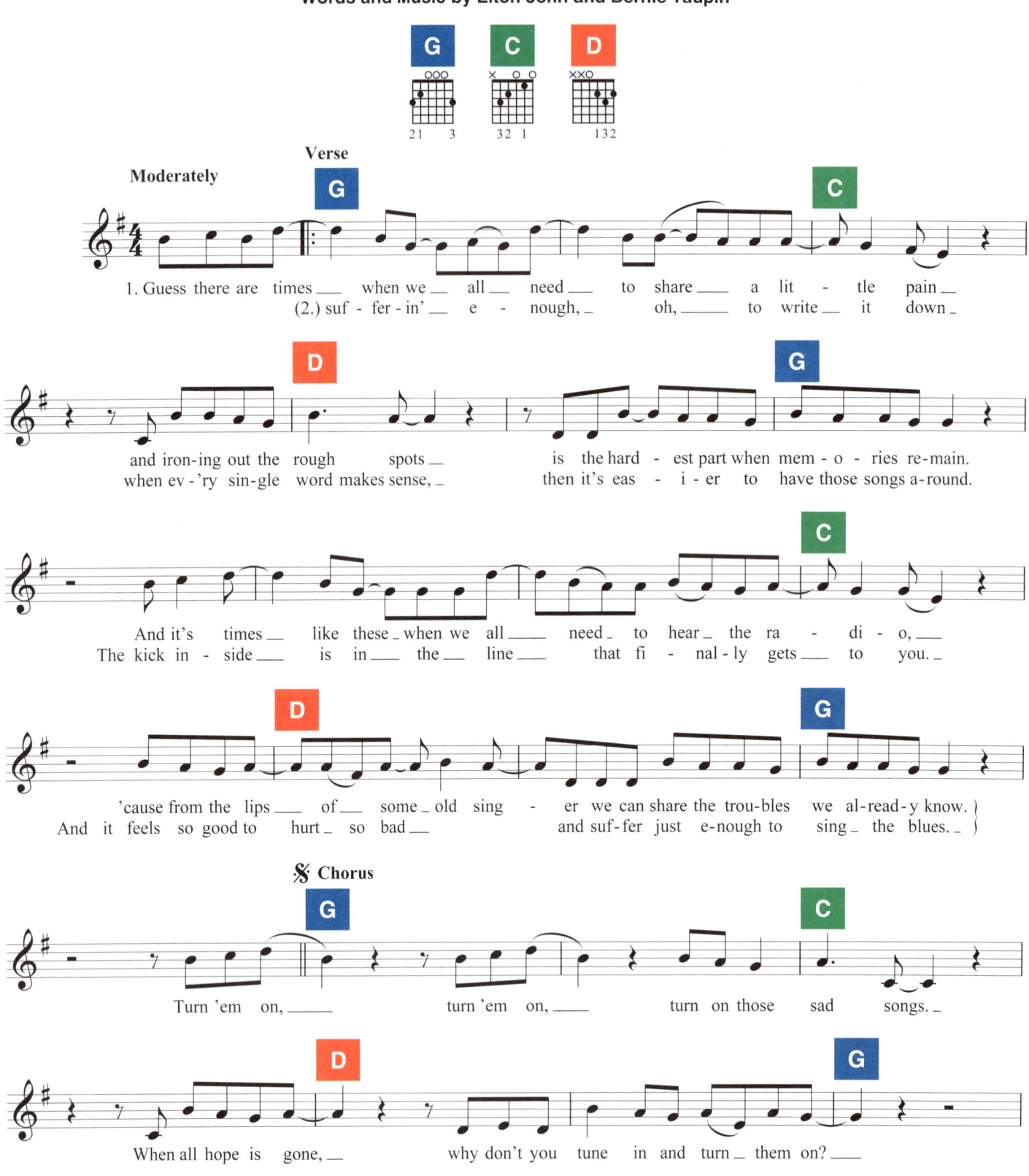

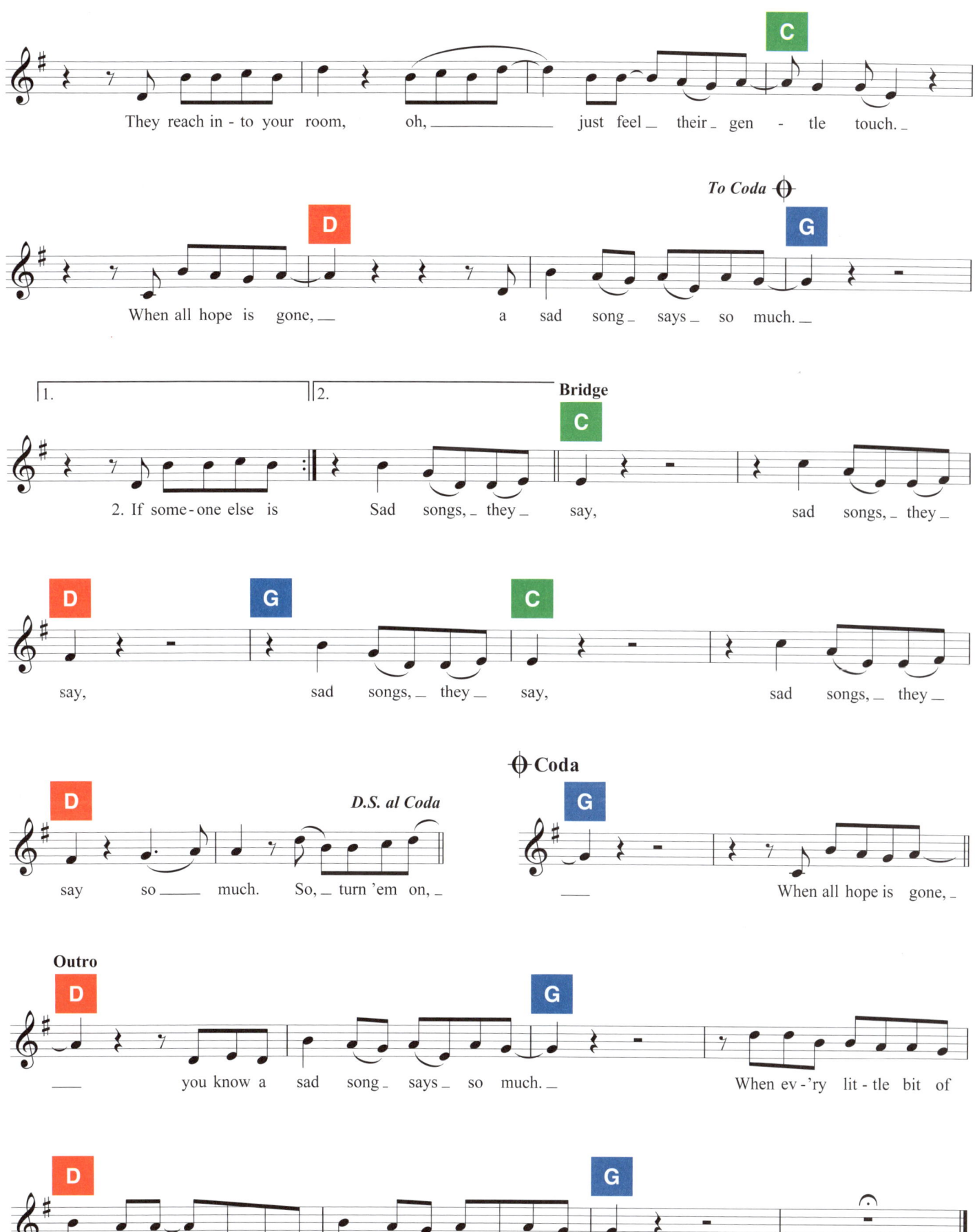

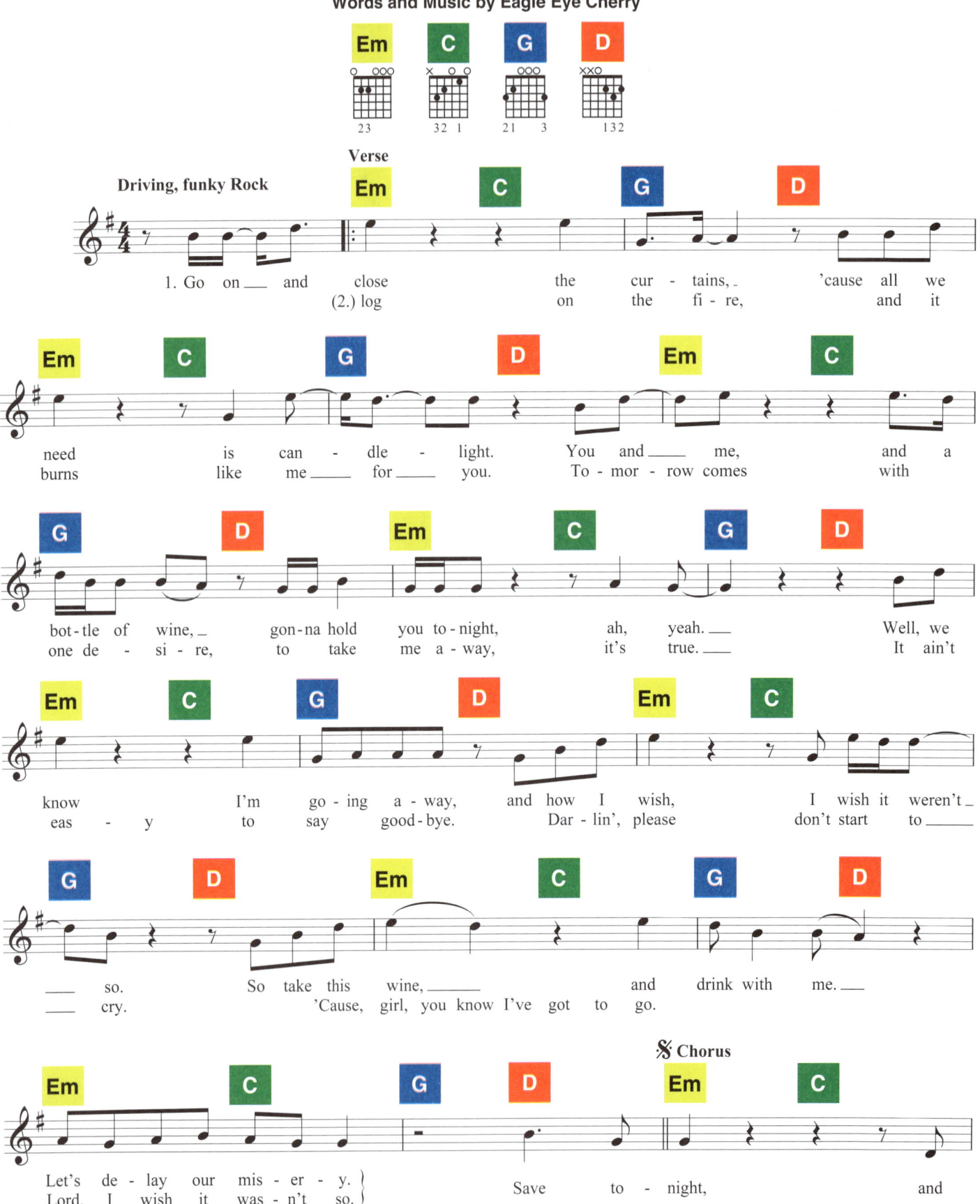

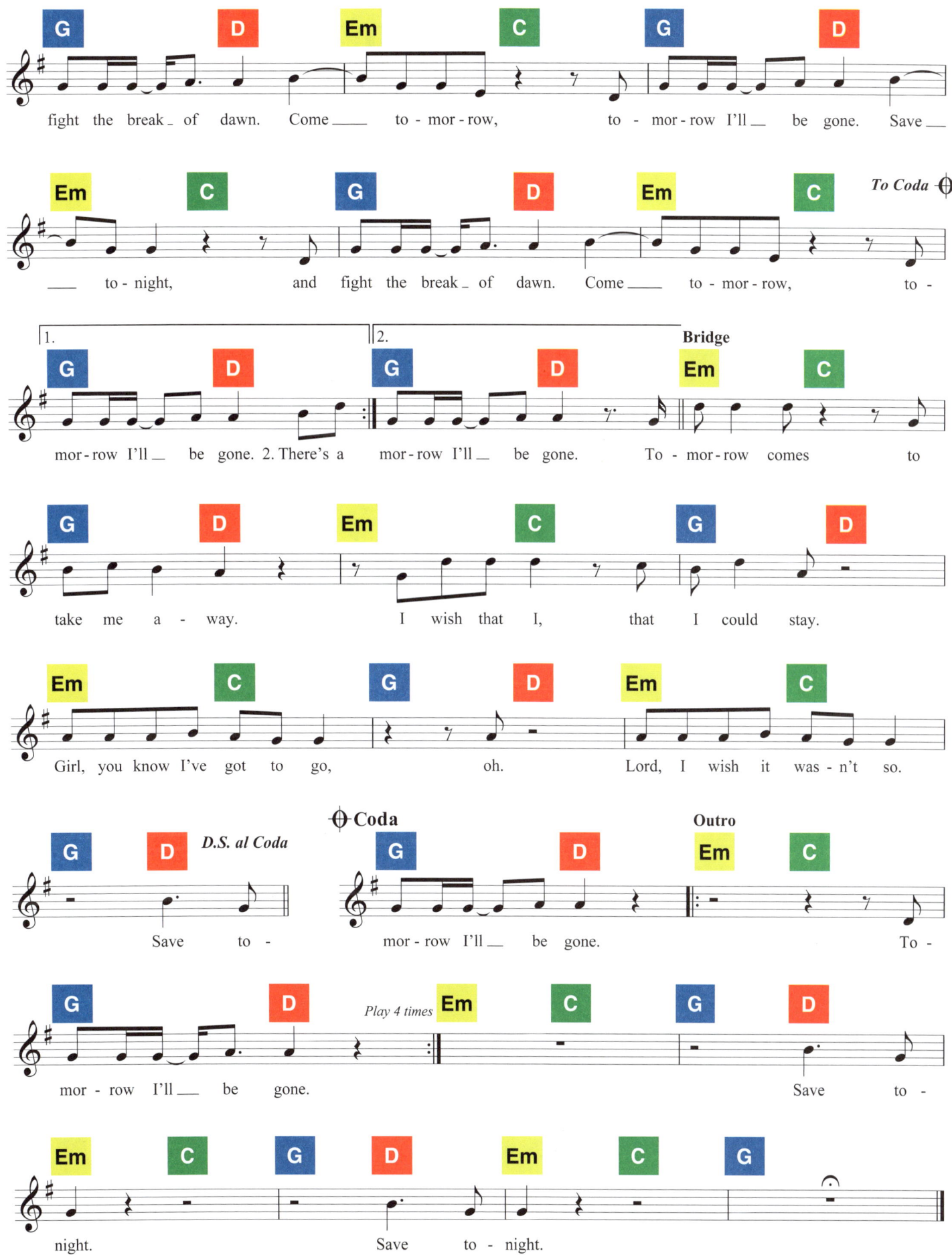

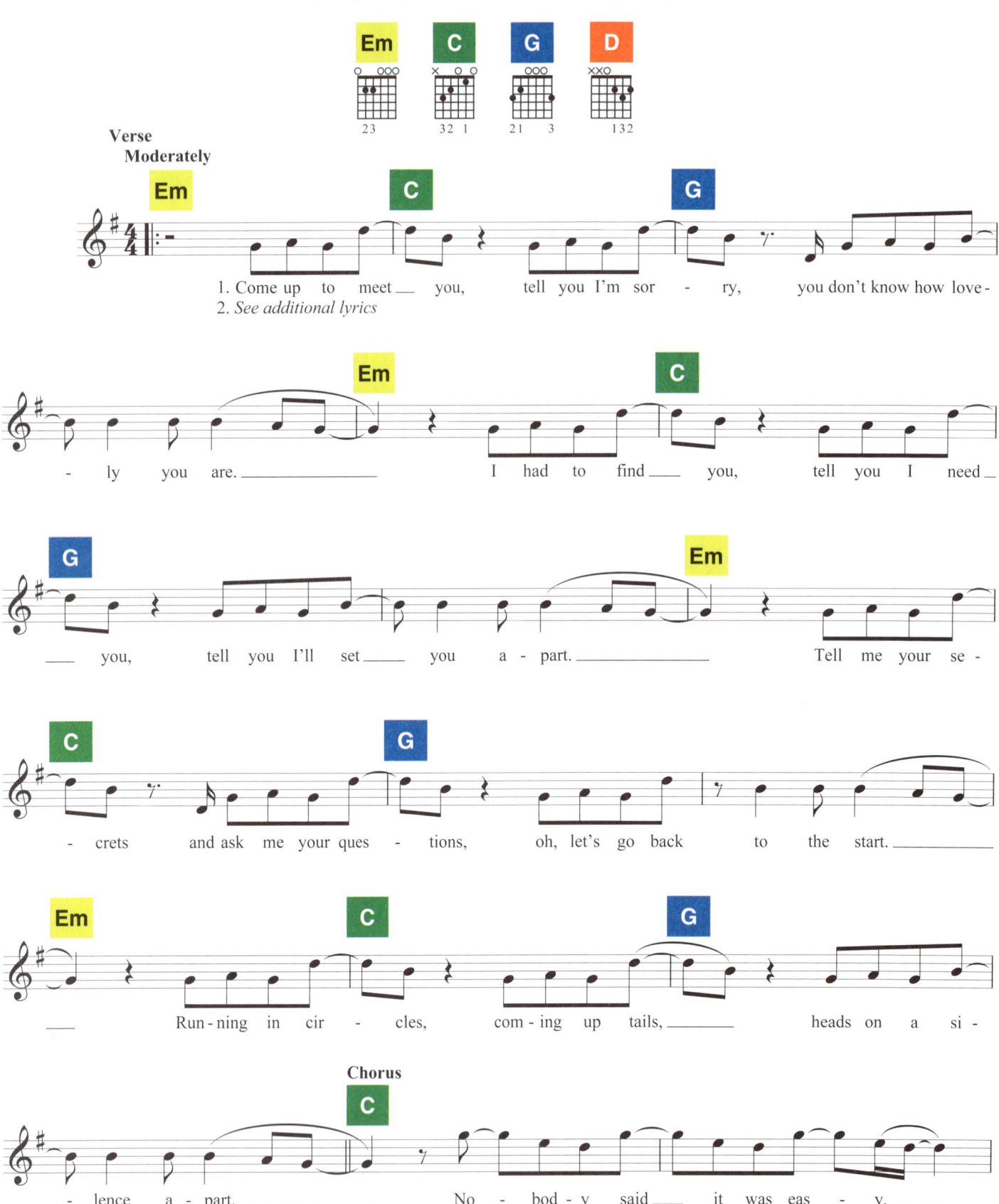

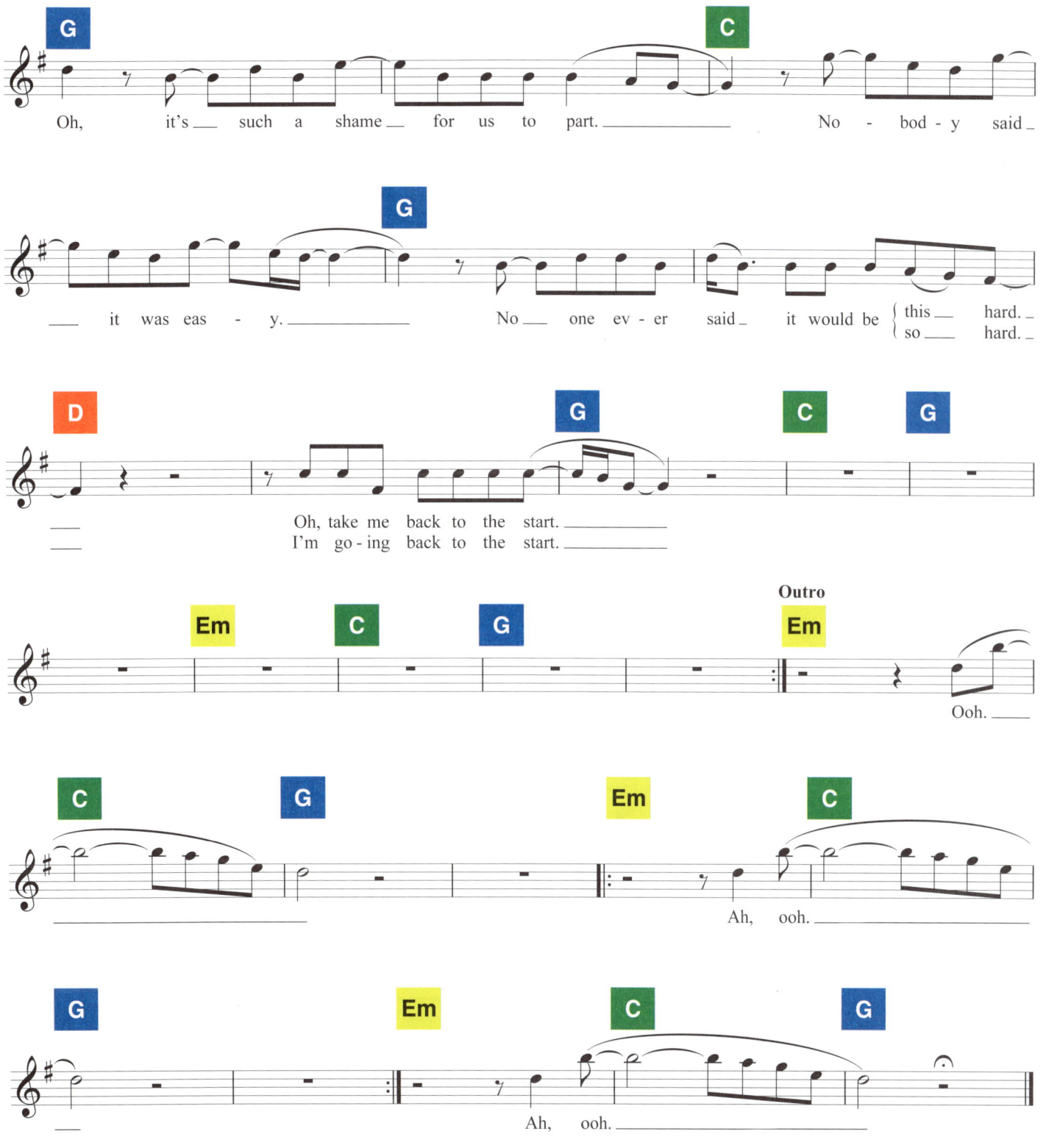

Additional Lyrics

2. I was just guessing at numbers and figures,
   Pulling the puzzles apart.
   Questions of science, science and progress
   Do not speak as loud as my heart.
   And tell me you love me, come back and haunt me.
   Oh, and I rush to the start.
   Running in circles, chasing our tails,
   Coming back as we are.

See You Later, Alligator

Words and Music by Robert Guidry

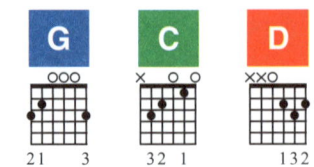

Additional Lyrics

2. When I thought of what she told me,
   Nearly made me lose my head.
   When I thought of what she told me,
   Nearly made me lose my head.
   But the next time that I saw her,
   Reminded her of what she said.

3. She said, I'm sorry, pretty daddy,
   You know my love is just for you.
   She said, I'm sorry, pretty daddy,
   You know my love is just for you.
   Won't you say that you'll forgive me,
   And say your love for me is true.

4. I said, wait a minute, 'gator,
   I know you meant it just for play.
   I said, wait a minute, 'gator,
   I know you meant it just for play.
   Don't you know you really hurt me,
   And this is what I have to say:

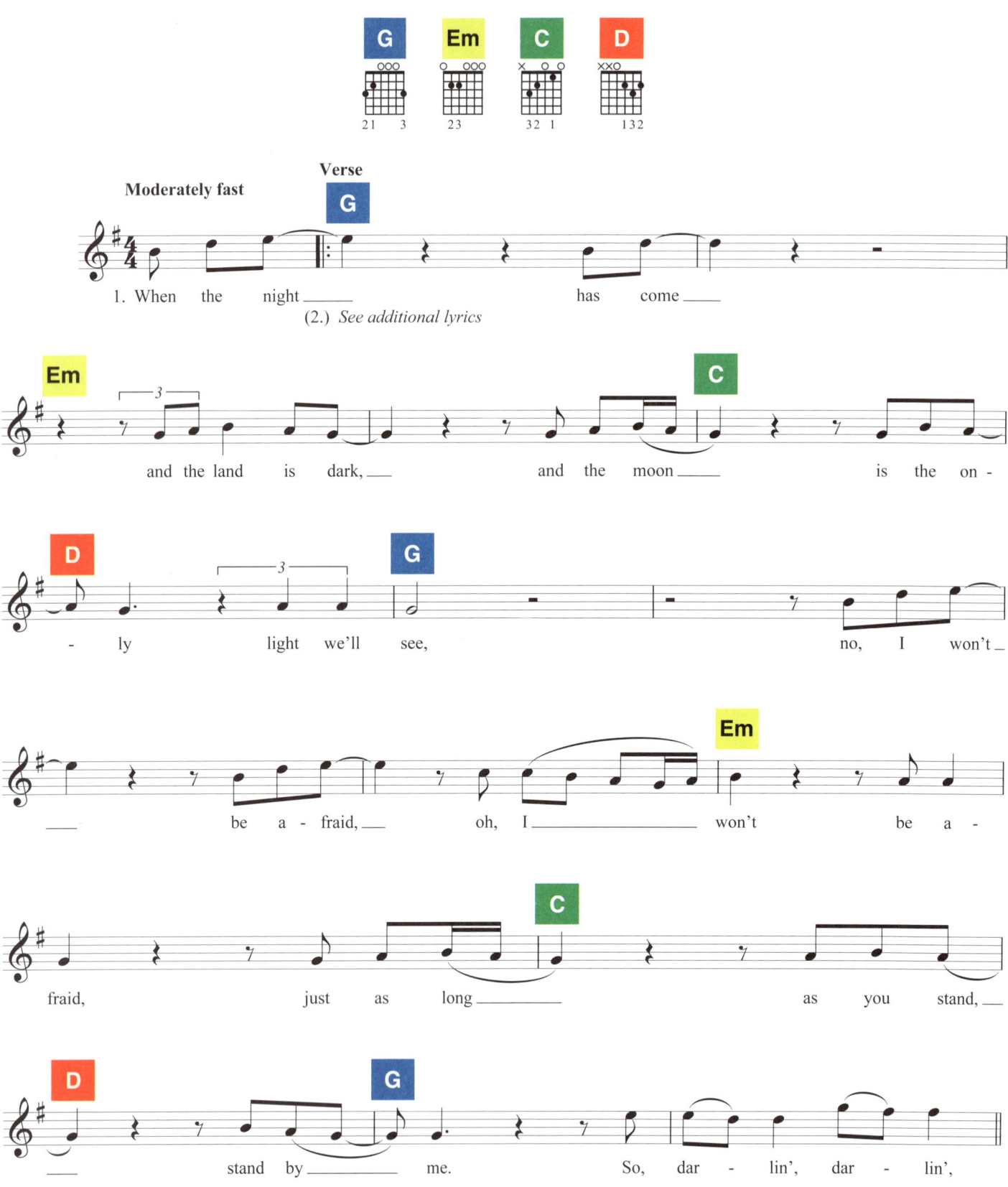

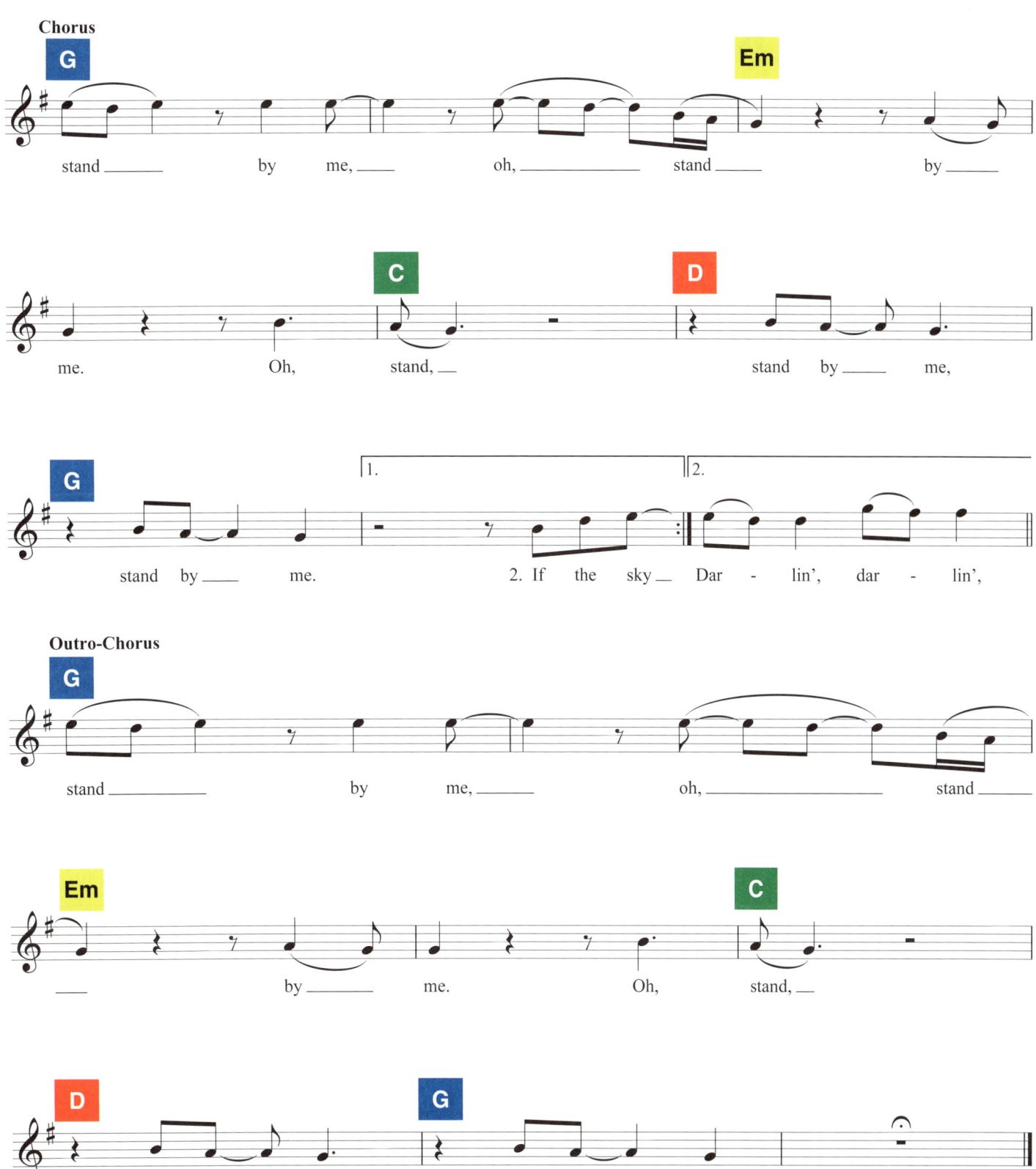

Additional Lyrics

2. If the sky that we look upon should tumble and fall,
Or the mountains should crumble to the sea,
I won't cry, I won't cry. No, I won't shed a tear,
Just as long as you stand, stand by me.
And darlin', darlin'… (*To Chorus*)

The Streets of Laredo
American Cowboy Song

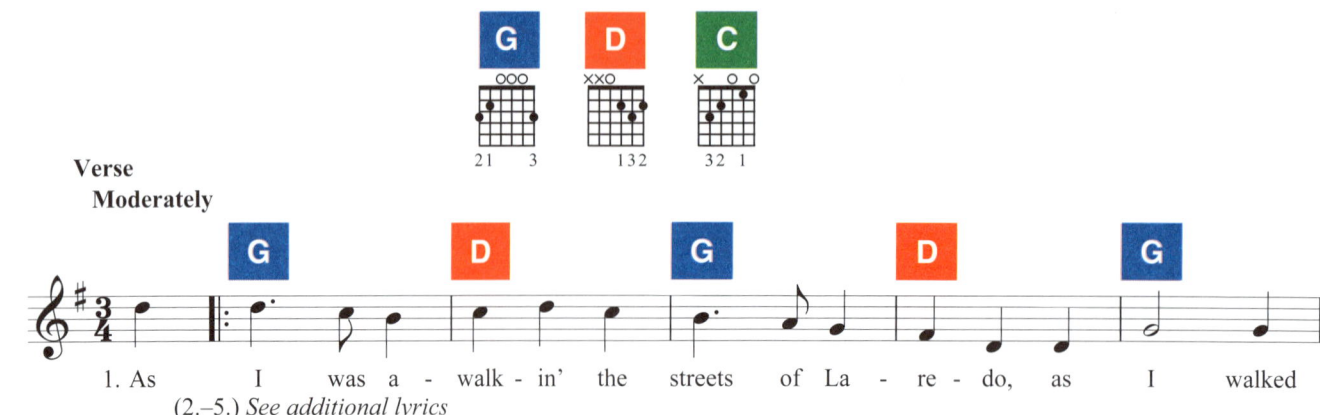

Verse
Moderately

1. As I was a-walkin' the streets of Laredo, as I walked
(2.–5.) *See additional lyrics*

out in Laredo one day, I spied a young cowboy all wrapped in white linen, all wrapped in white linen and cold as the clay. 2. "I fall."

Additional Lyrics

2. "I see by your outfit that you are a cowboy,"
   These words he did say as I boldly walked by.
   "Come sit down beside me and hear my sad story.
   I'm shot in the breast and I know I must die."

3. "It was once in the saddle I used to go dashing,
   Once in the saddle I used to go gay.
   First down to Rosie's and then to the card house.
   Got shot in the breast and I'm dying today."

4. "Get sixteen gamblers to carry my coffin,
   Let six jolly cowboys come sing me a song.
   Take me to the graveyard and lay the sod o'er me,
   For I'm a young cowboy and I know I've done wrong."

5. "Oh, bang the drum slowly and play the fife lowly,
   Play the dead march as you carry me along.
   Put bunches of roses all over my coffin,
   Roses to deaden the clods as they fall."

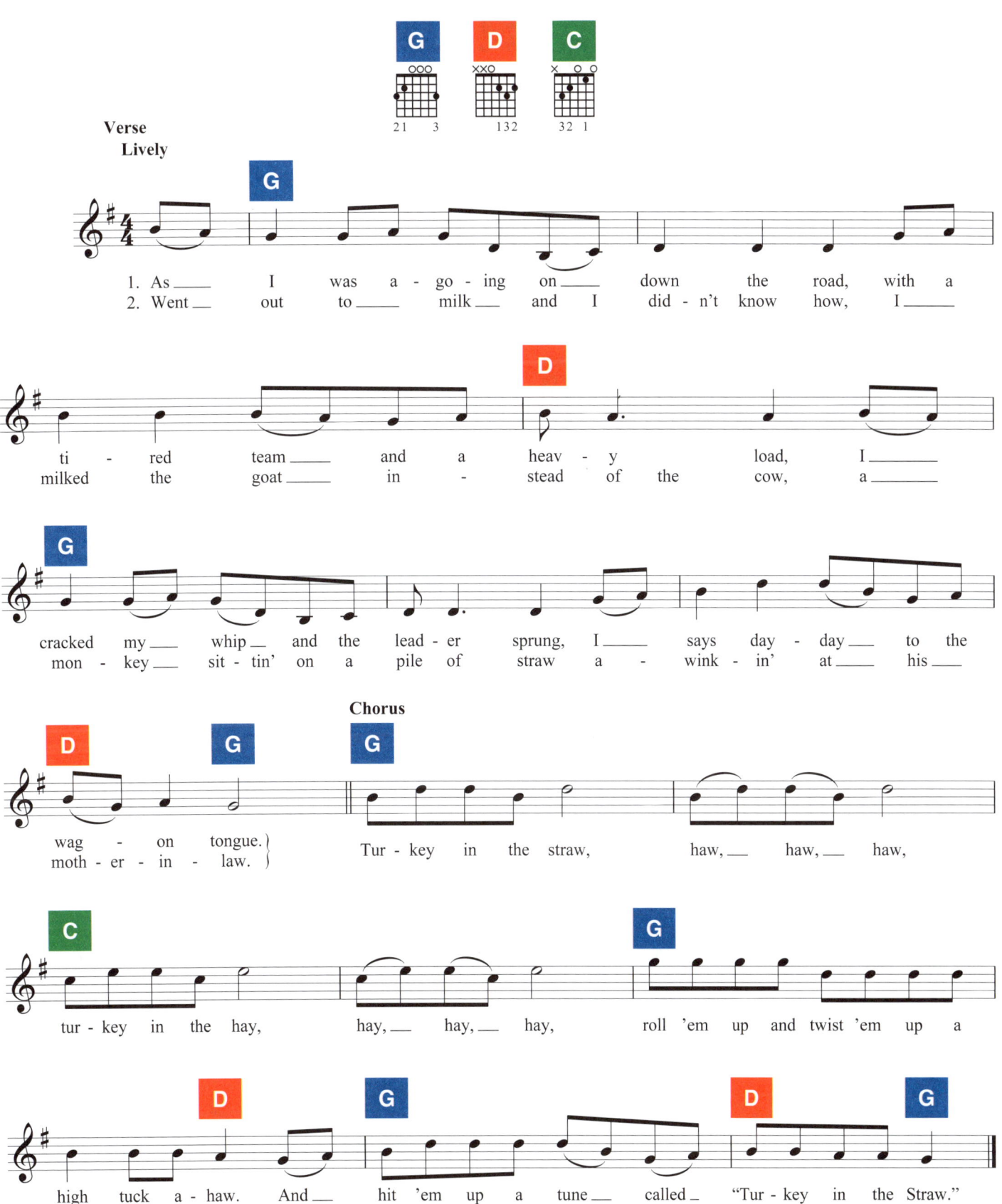

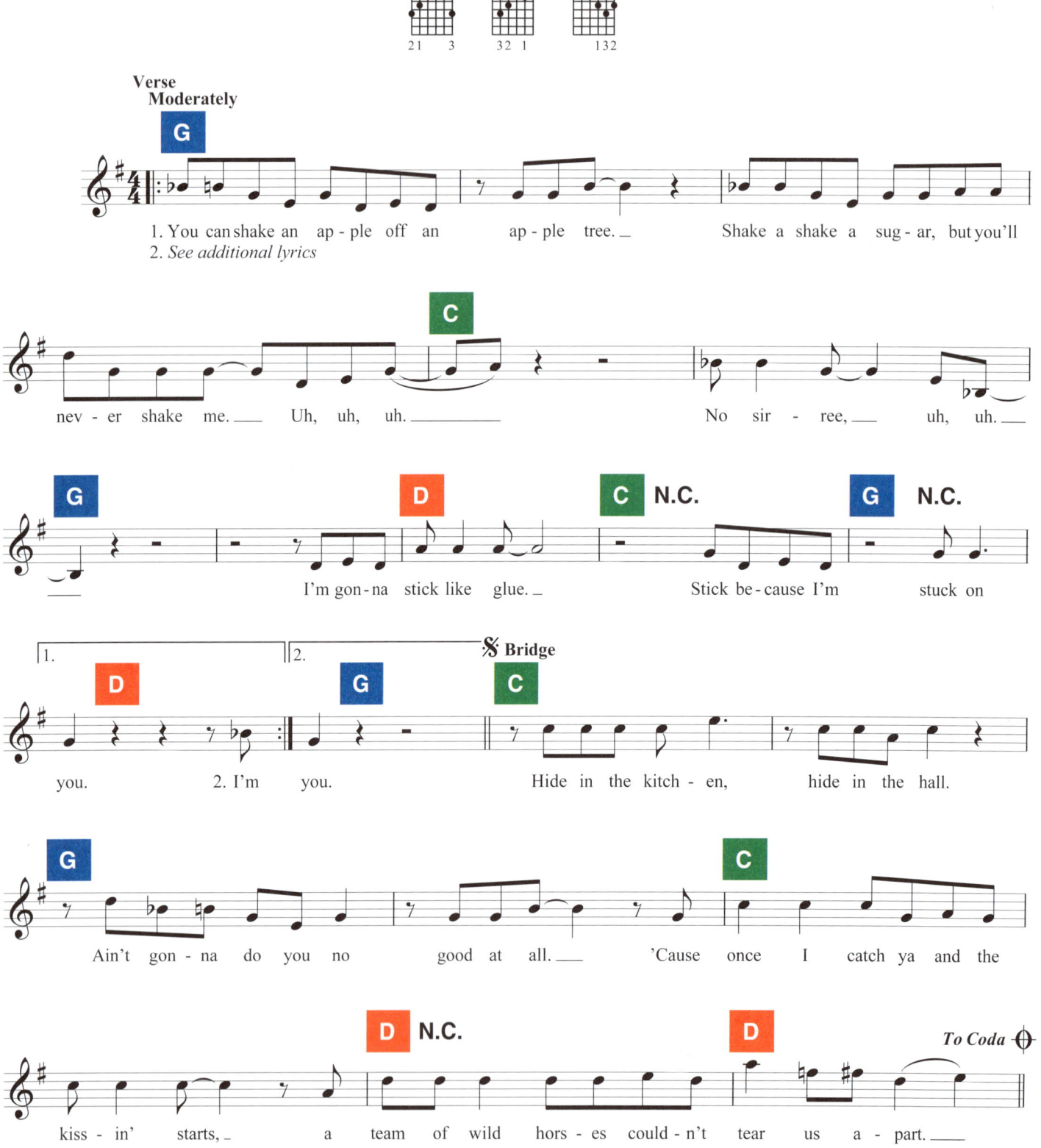

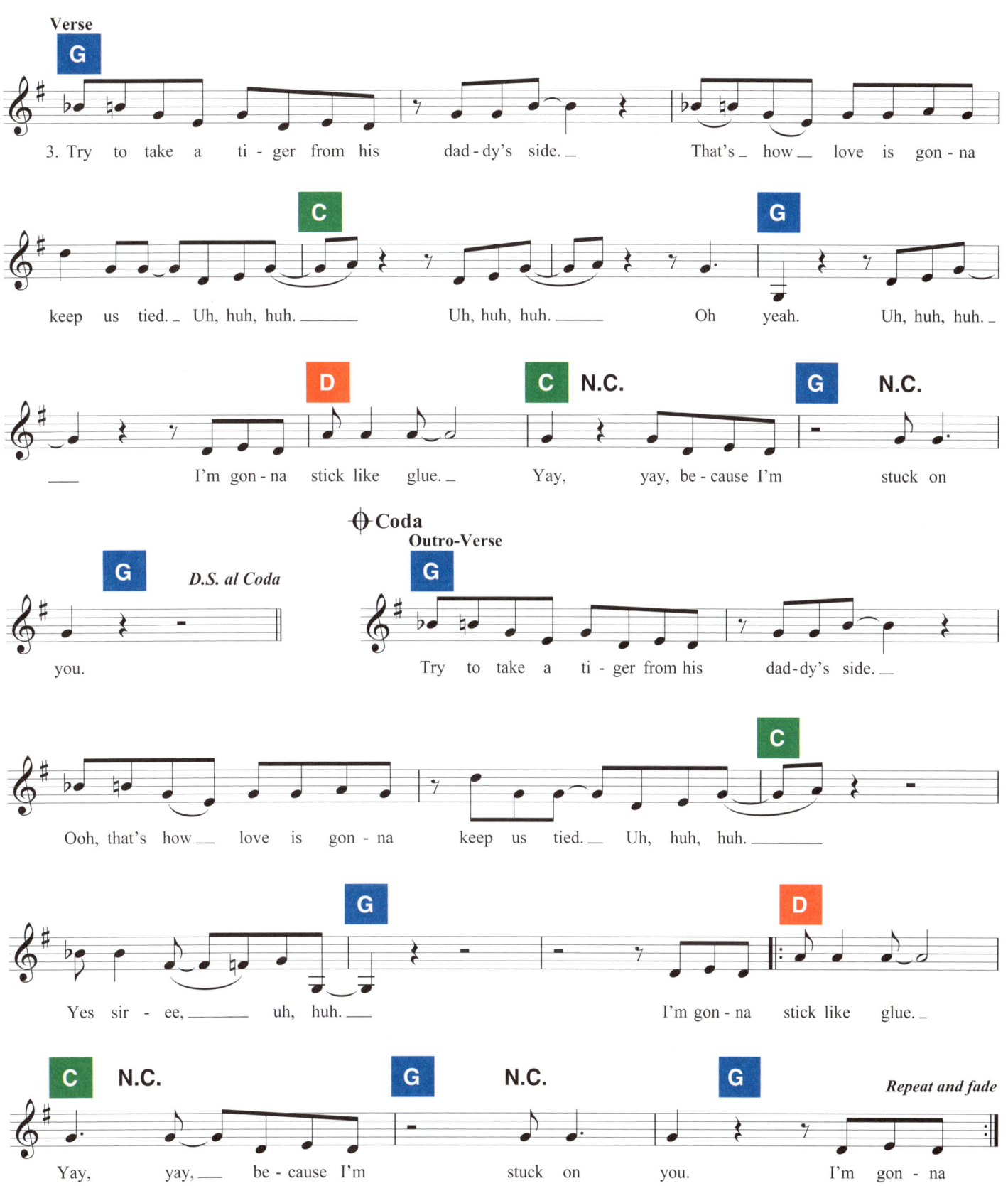

Additional Lyrics

2. I'm gonna squeeze my fingers through your long black hair,
   Squeeze you tighter than a grizzly bear.
   Uh, huh, huh. Yes siree, uh, huh.
   I'm gonna stick like glue.
   Stick because I'm stuck on you.

Sugar, Sugar

Words and Music by Andy Kim and Jeff Barry

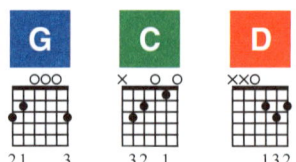

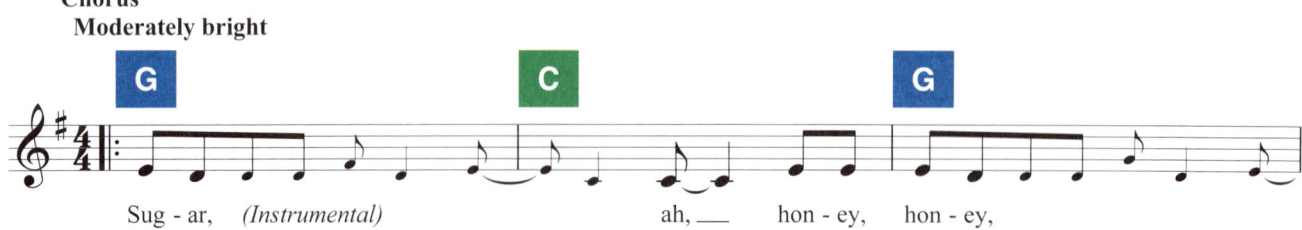

Sug-ar, (Instrumental) ah, __ hon-ey, hon-ey,

you are my can-dy girl __ and you've got me

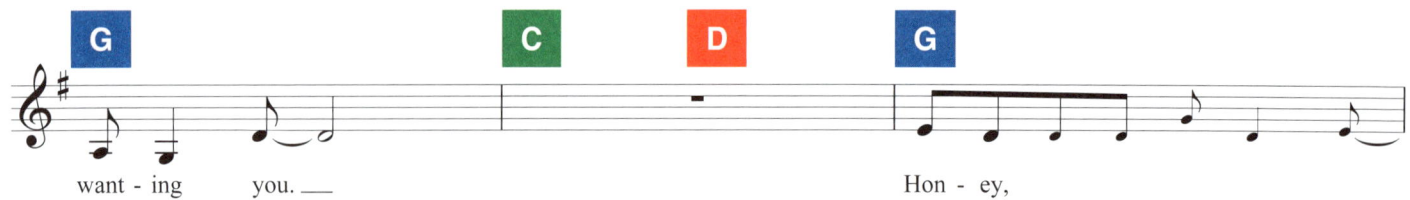

want-ing you. __ Hon-ey,

ah, __ sug-ar, sug-ar, you are my

can-dy girl __ and you've got me want-ing you. __

Copyright © 1969 Sony/ATV Music Publishing LLC and Steeplechase Music
Copyright Renewed
All Rights on behalf of Sony/ATV Music Publishing LLC Administered by
Sony/ATV Music Publishing LLC, 424 Church Street, Suite 1200, Nashville, TN 37219
International Copyright Secured   All Rights Reserved

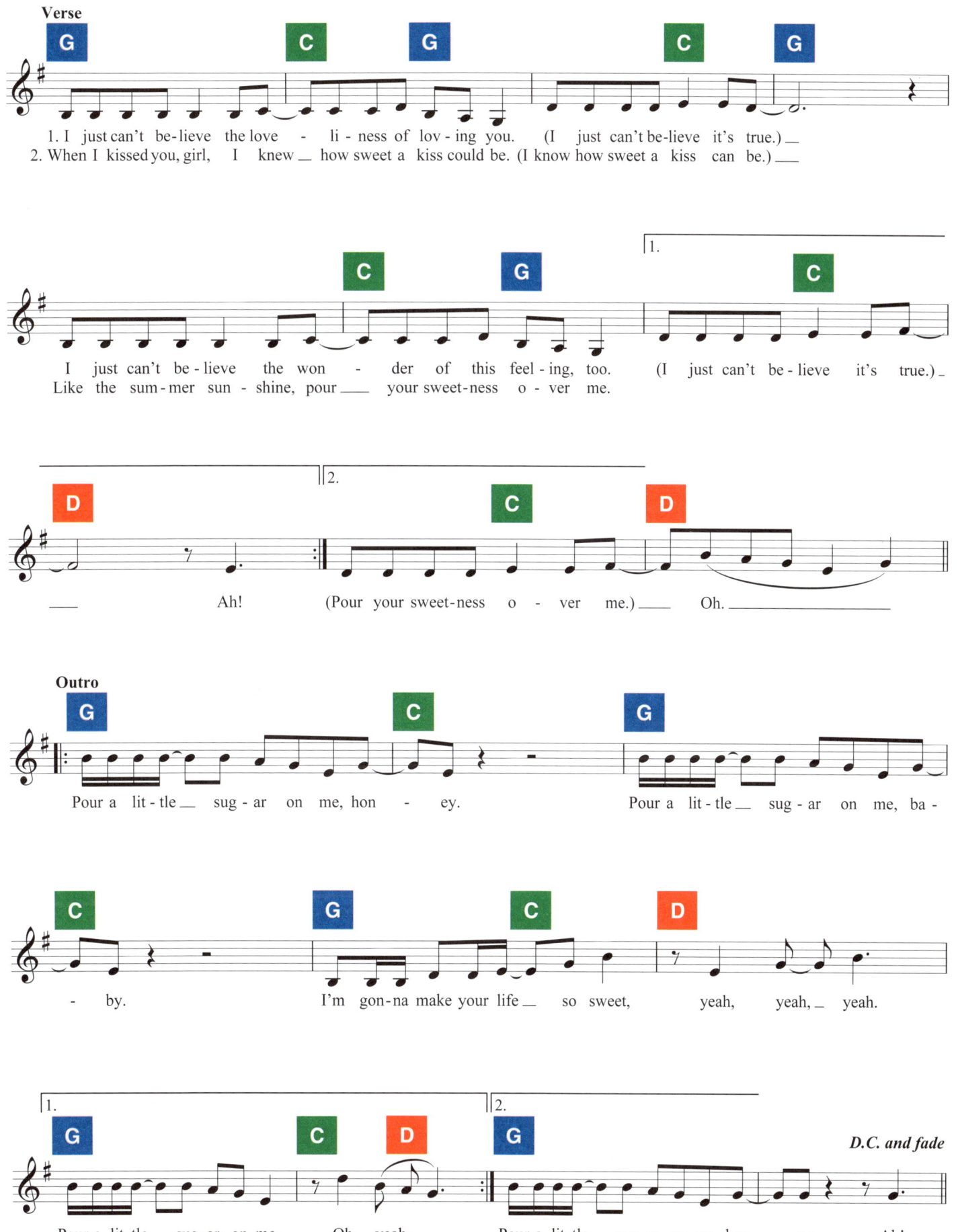

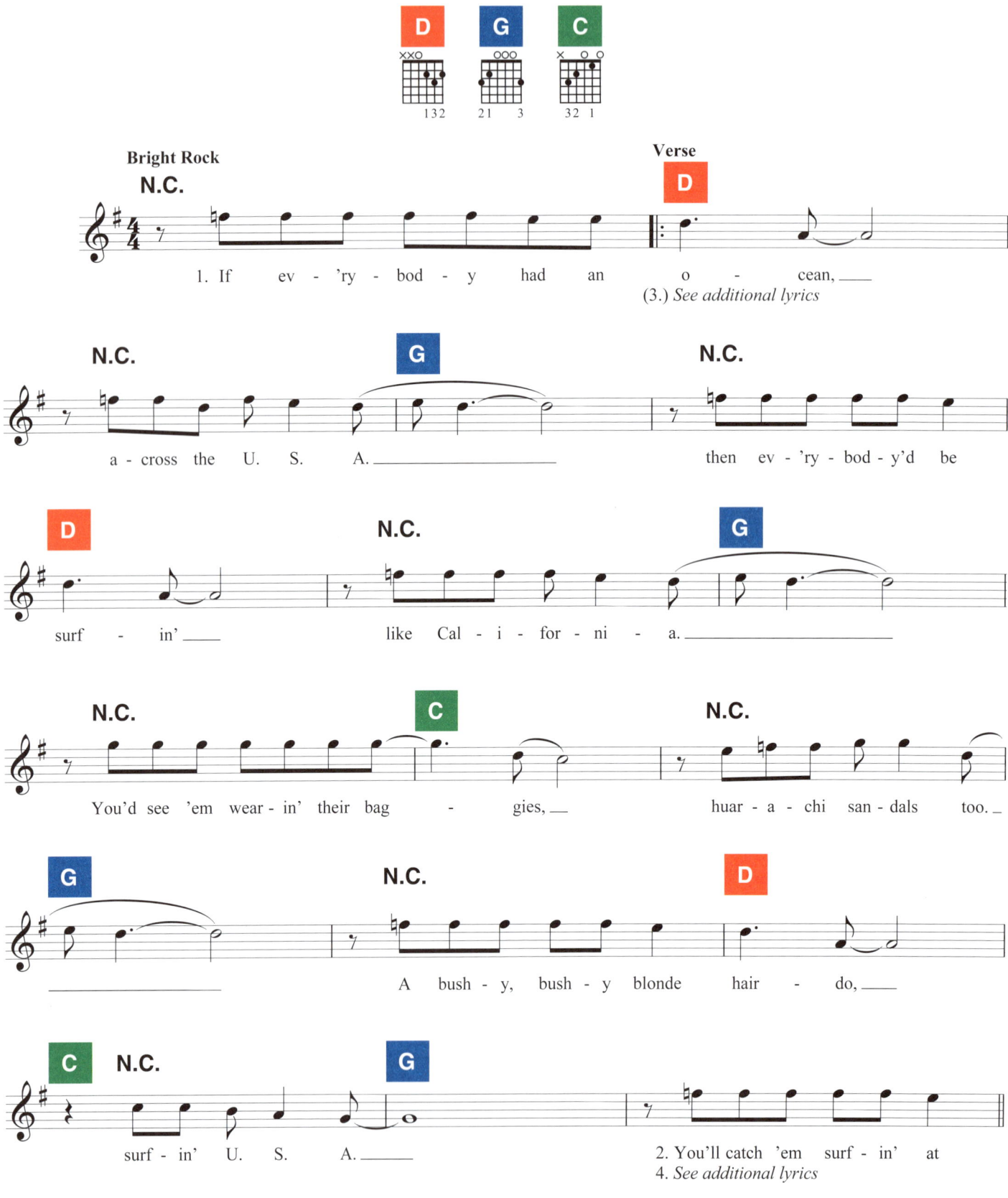

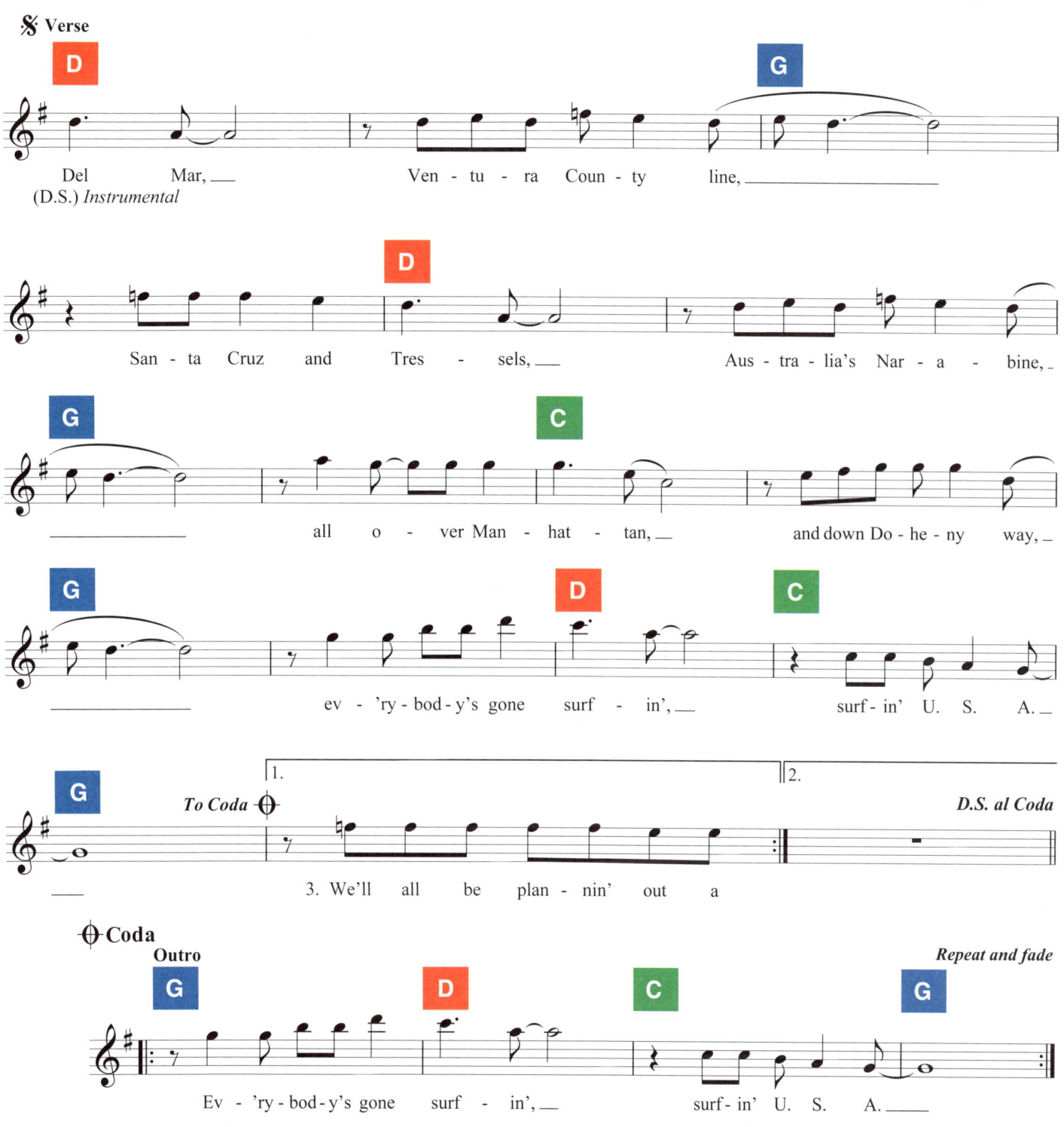

Additional Lyrics

3. We'll all be plannin' out a route we're gonna take real soon.
We're waxin' down our surfboards, we can't wait for June.
We'll all be gone for the summer, we're on safari to stay.
Tell the teacher we're surfin', surfin' U.S.A.

4. At Haggarty's and Swami's, Pacific Palisades,
San Onofre and Sunset, Redondo Beach, L.A.,
All over La Jolla, at Waiamea Bay,
Ev'rybody's gone surfin', surfin' U.S.A.

Sweet Home Chicago

Words and Music by Robert Johnson

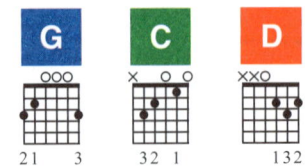

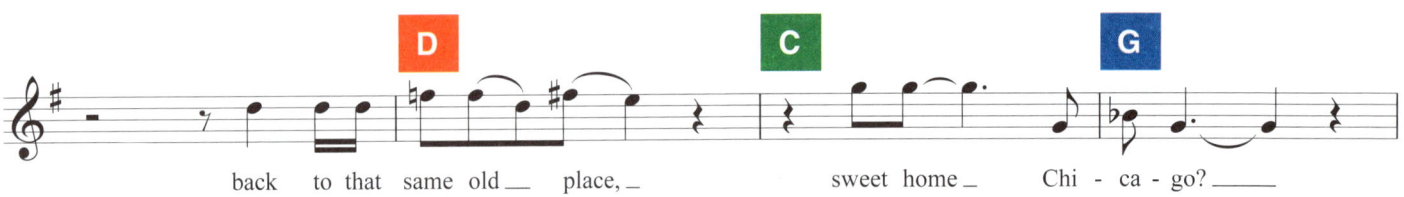

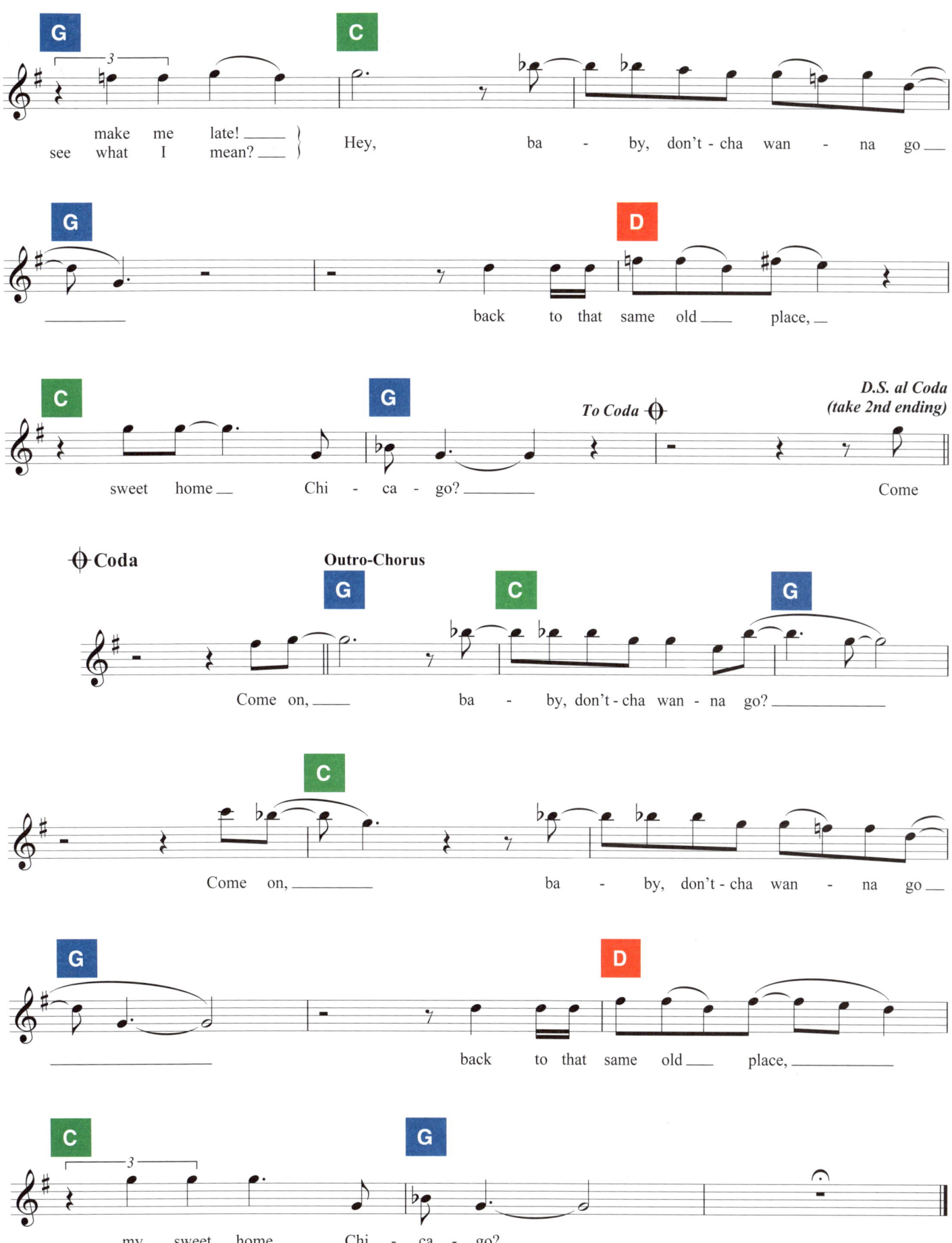

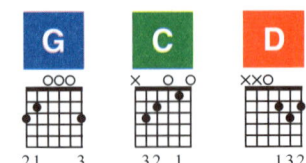

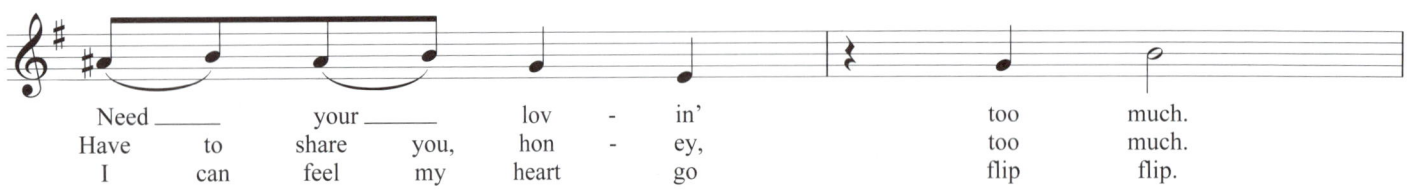
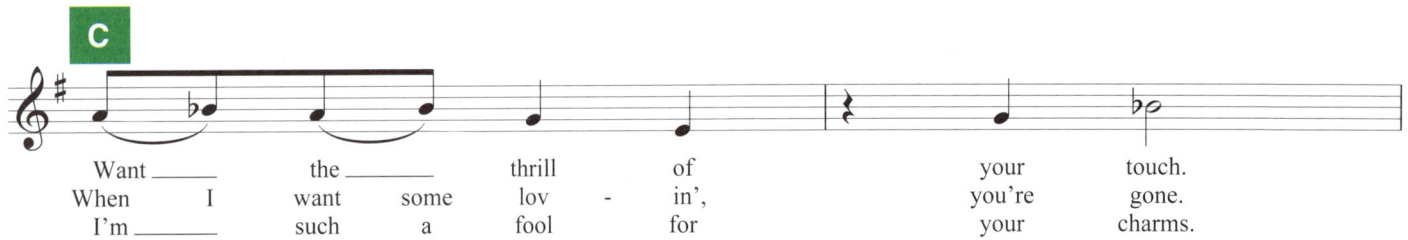

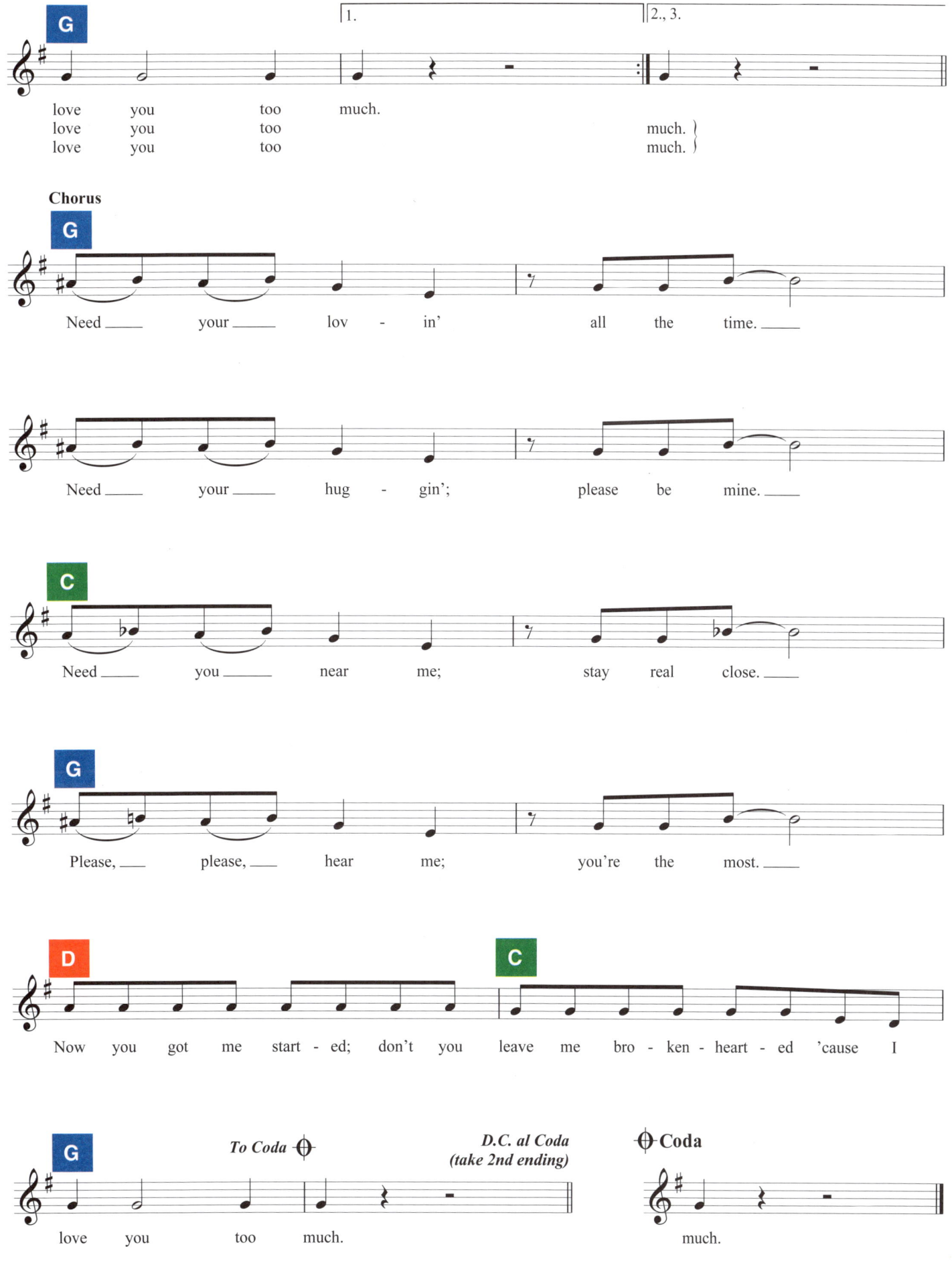

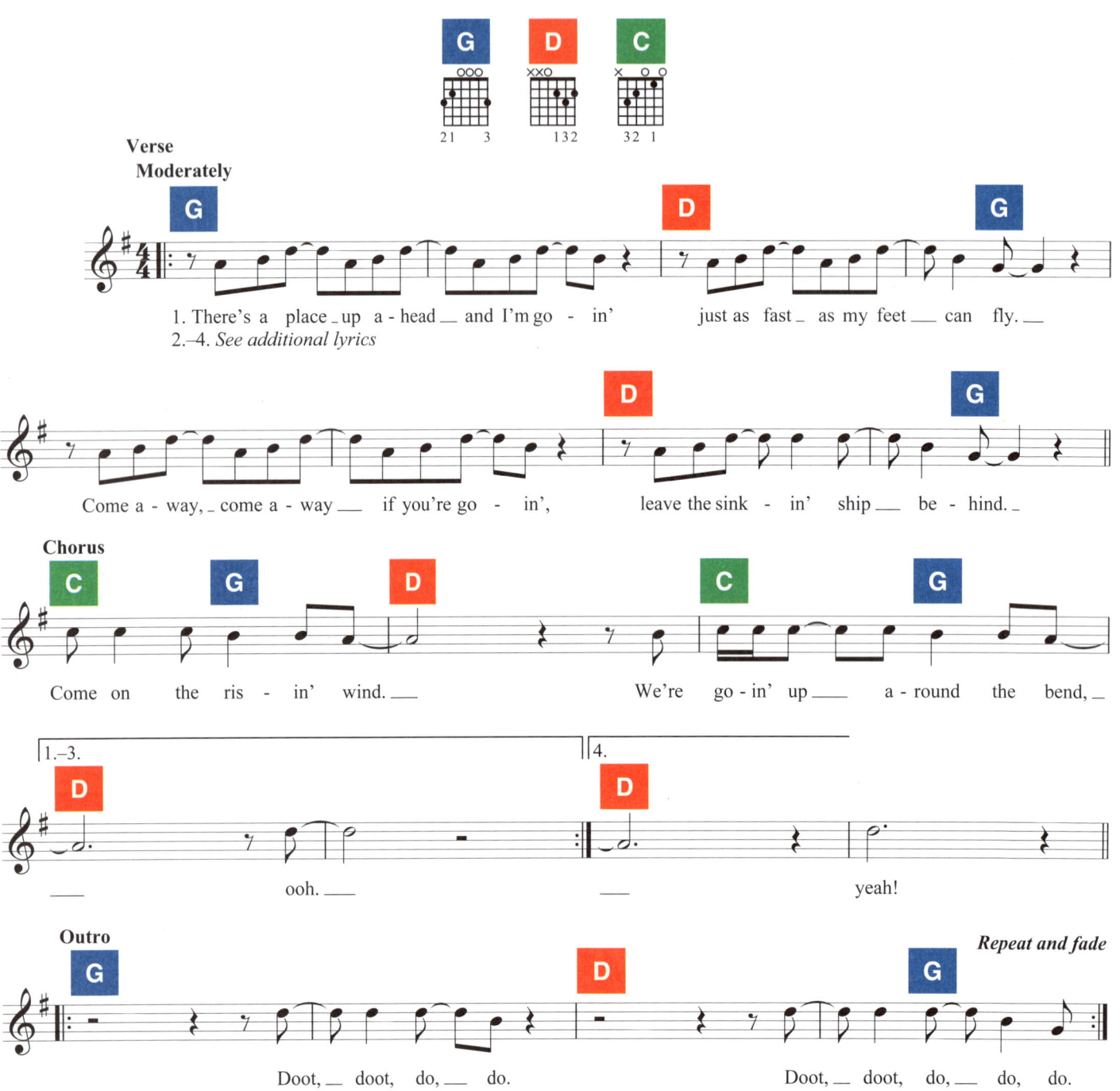

Additional Lyrics

2. Bring a song and a smile for the banjo.
   Better get while the gettin's good.
   Hitch a ride to end of the highway
   Where the neons turn to wood.

3. You can ponder perpetual motion,
   Fix your mind on a crystal day.
   Always time for a good conversation,
   There's an ear for what you say.

4. Catch a ride to the end of the highway
   And we'll meet by the big red tree.
   There's a place up ahead and I'm goin'.
   Come along, come along with me.

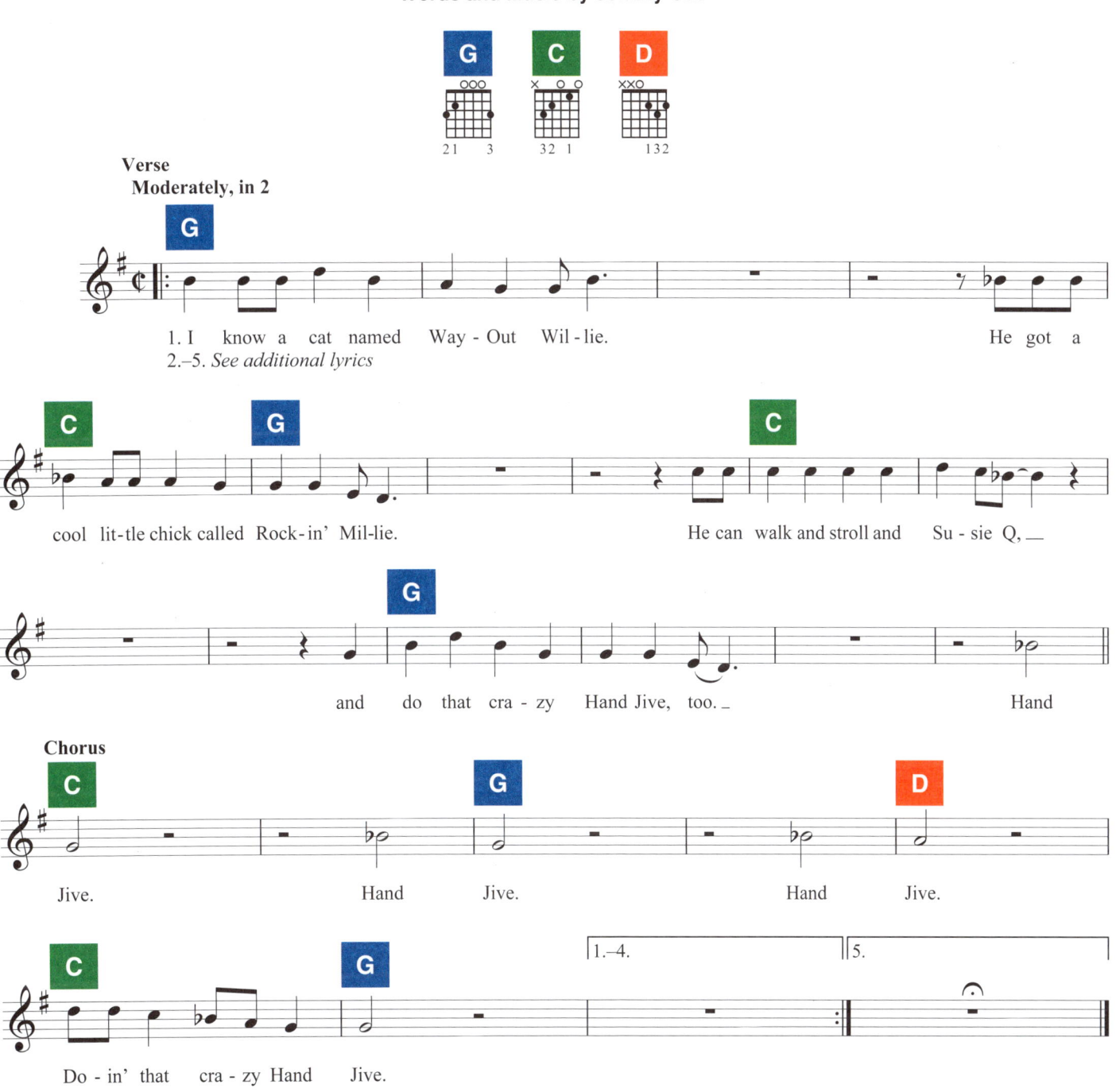

When You Say Nothing at All

Words and Music by Don Schlitz and Paul Overstreet

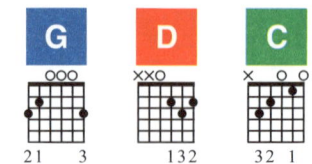

1. It's a-maz-ing how you can speak right to my heart.
2. *See additional lyrics*

With-out say-ing a word, you can light up the dark.

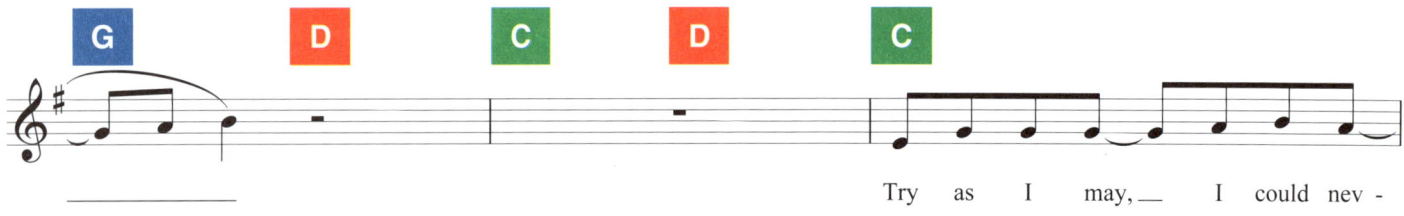

Try as I may, I could nev-

-er ex-plain what I hear when you don't say a thing. The

% **Chorus**

smile on your face lets me know that you need me. There's a truth in your eyes say-ing you'll

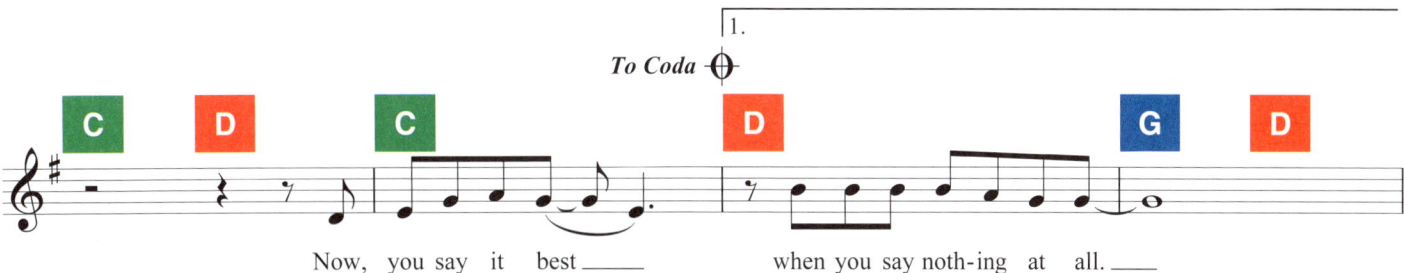
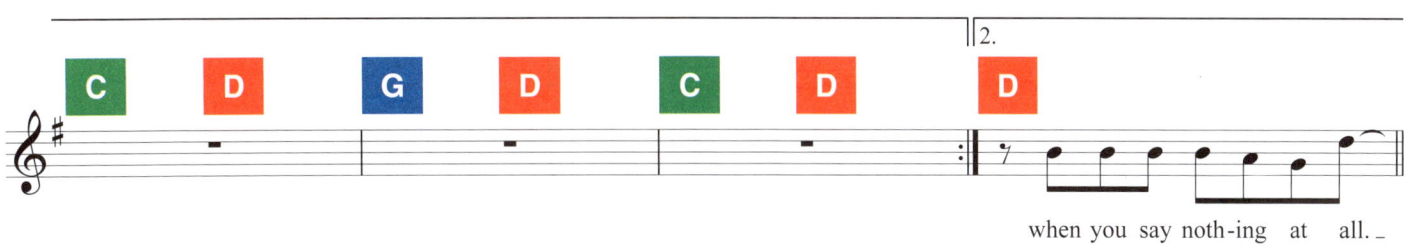
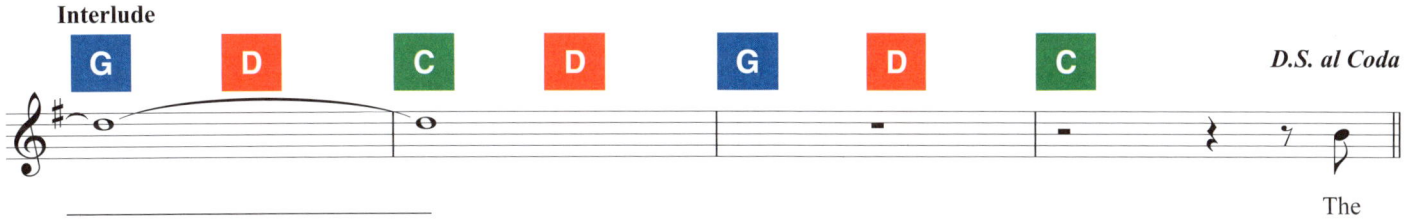
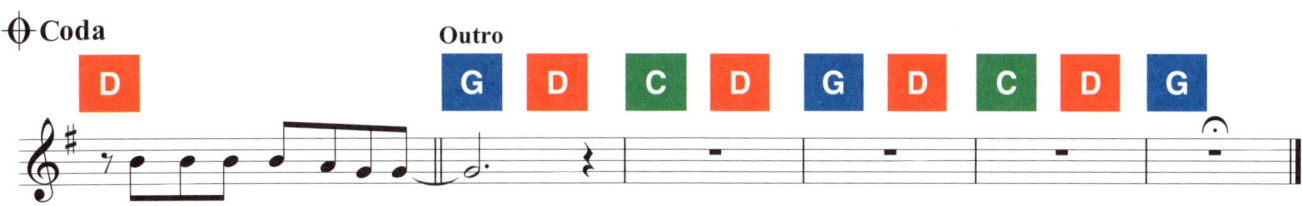

Additional Lyrics

2. All day long I can hear people talking out loud.
   But when you hold me near, you drown out the crowd.
   Old Mister Webster could never define
   What's being said between your heart and mine.

Yakety Yak

Words and Music by Jerry Leiber and Mike Stoller

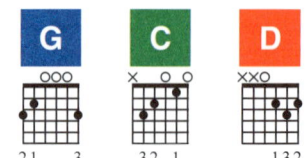

Copyright © 1958 Sony/ATV Music Publishing LLC
Copyright Renewed
All Rights Administered by Sony/ATV Music Publishing LLC, 424 Church Street, Suite 1200, Nashville, TN 37219
International Copyright Secured   All Rights Reserved

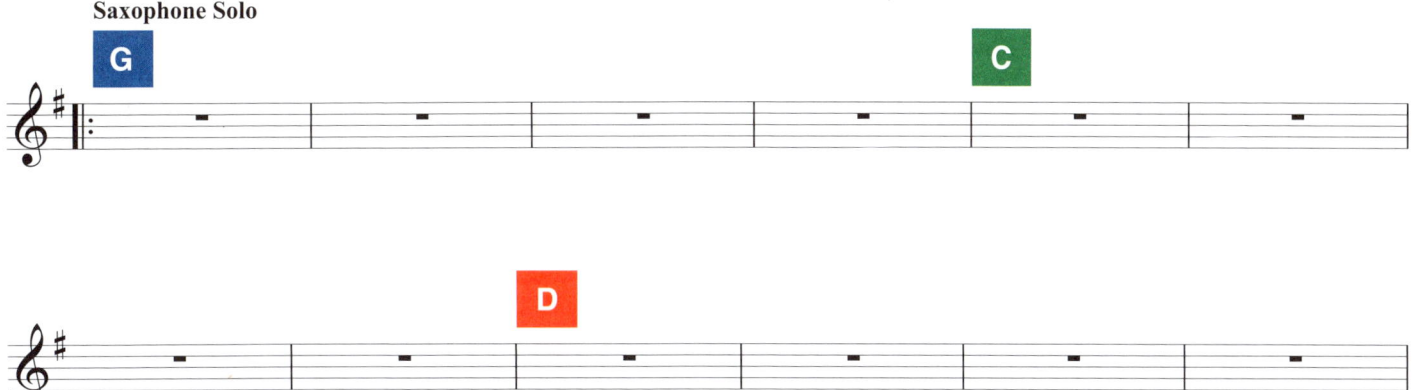
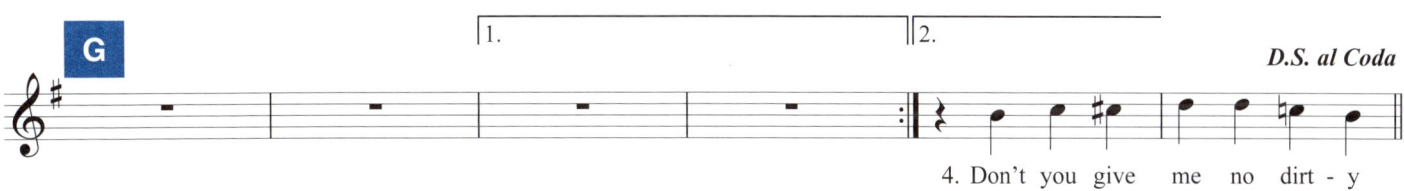
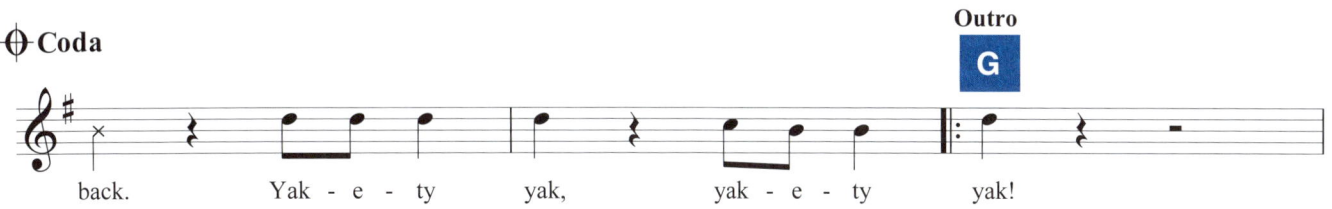

Additional Lyrics

2. Just finish cleanin' up your room.
   Let's see that dust fly with that broom.
   Get all that garbage out of sight,
   Or you don't go out Friday night.
   Yakety yak! *(Spoken:) Don't talk back.*

3. You just put on your coat and hat,
   And walk yourself to the laundromat.
   And when you finish doing that,
   Bring in the dog and put out the cat.
   Yakety yak! *(Spoken:) Don't talk back.*

4. Don't you give me no dirty looks.
   Your father's hip; he knows what cooks.
   Just tell your hoodlum friends outside,
   You ain't got time to take a ride.
   Yakety yak! *(Spoken:) Don't talk back.*

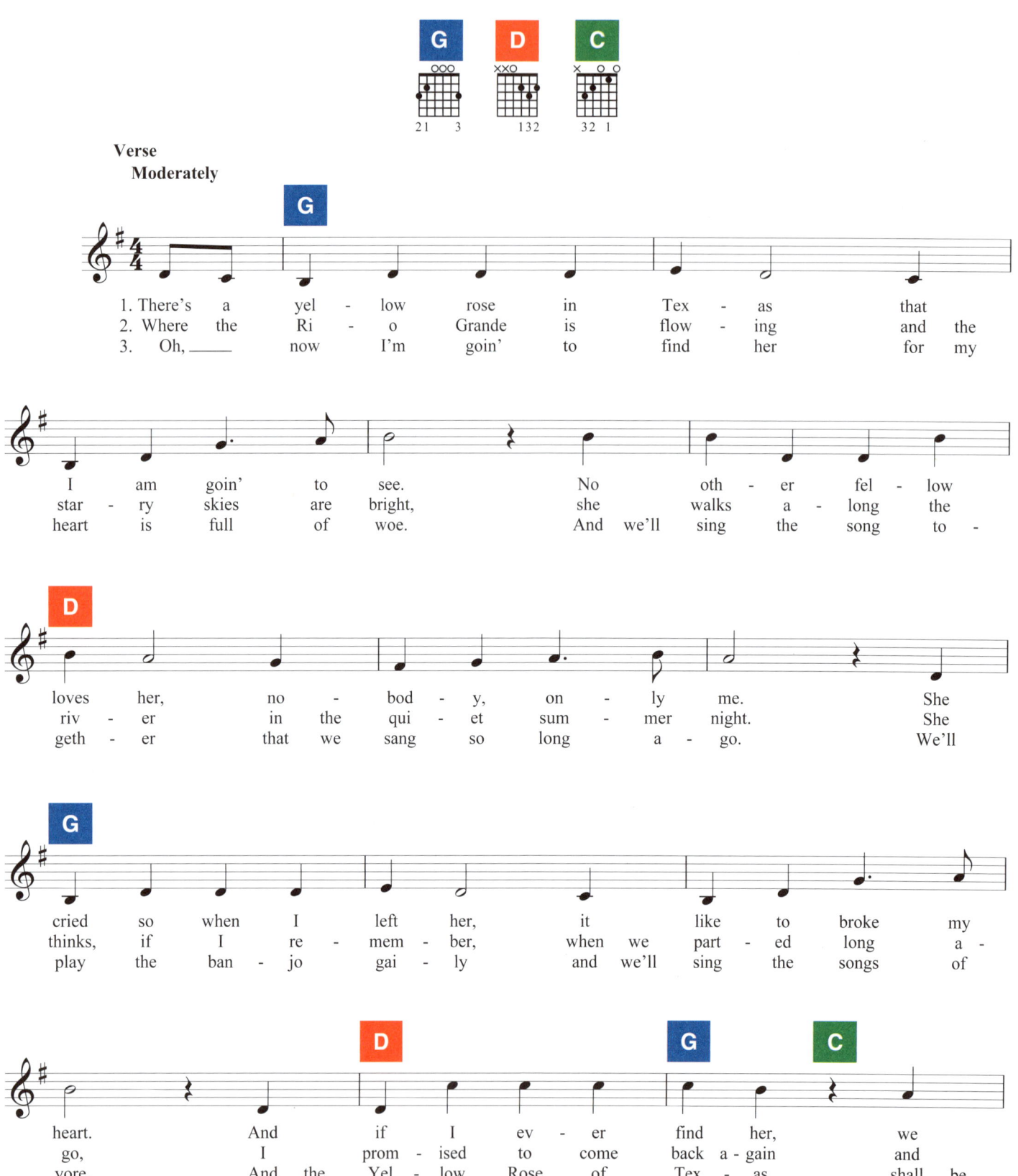

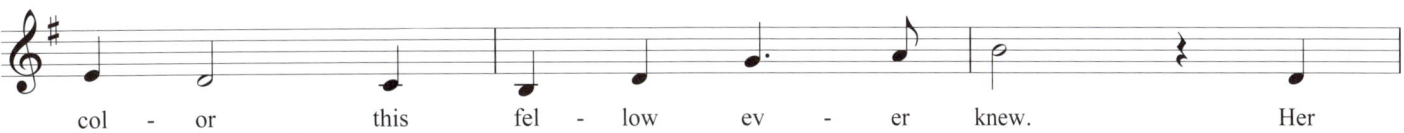

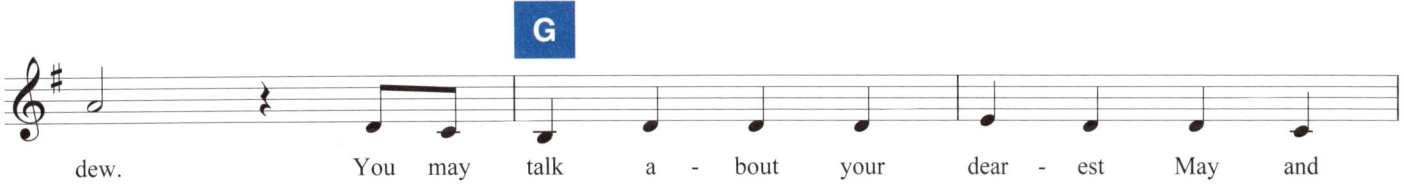
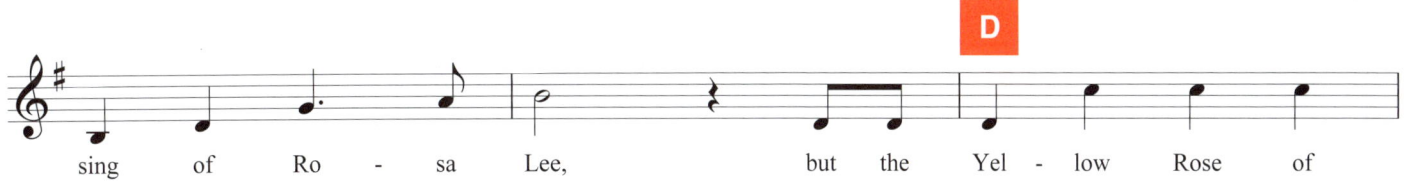
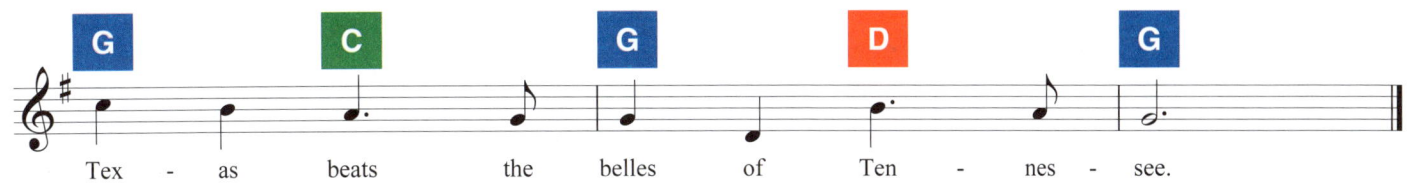

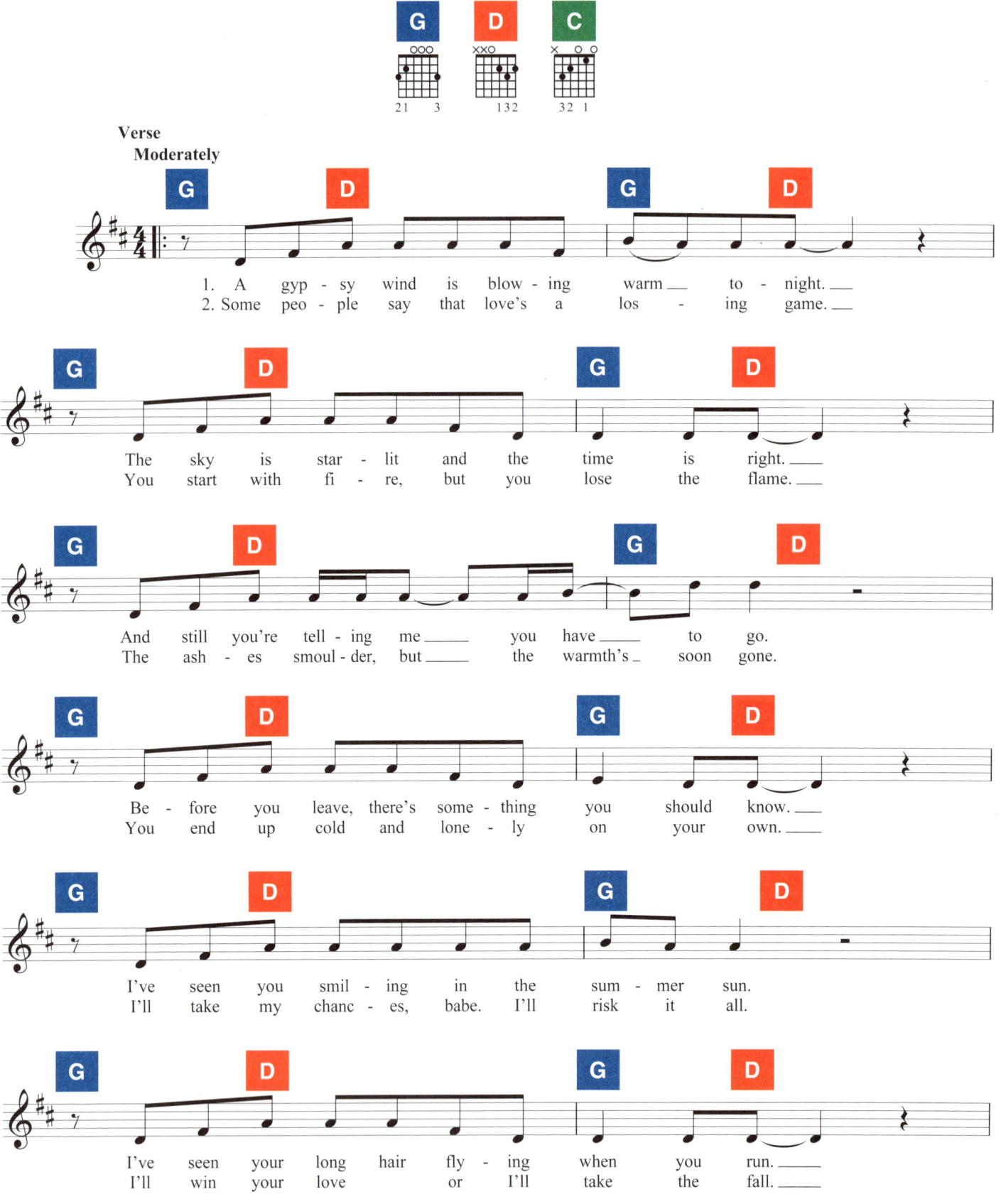

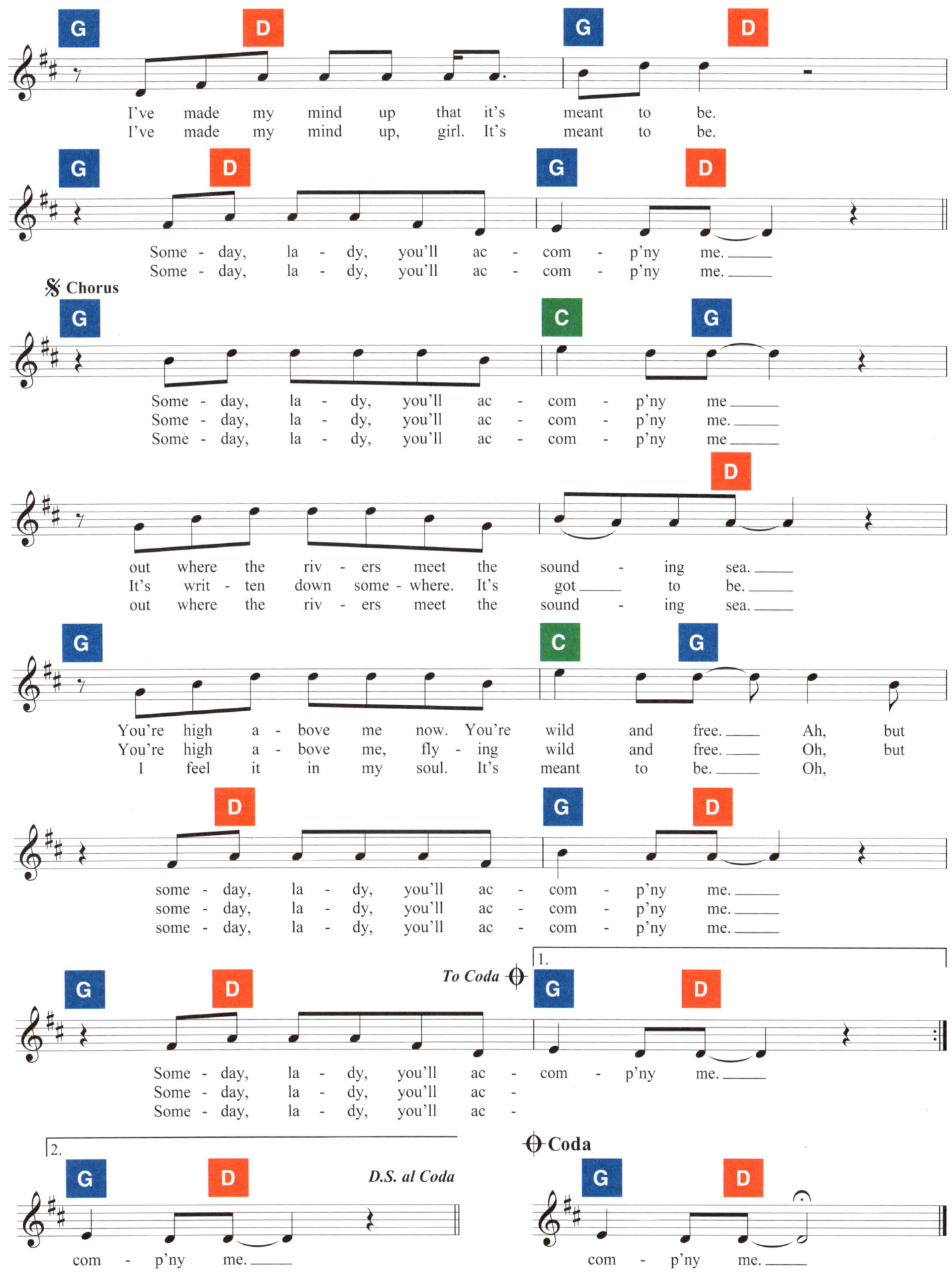

STRUM AND PICK PATTERNS

This chart contains various patterns that can be used with songs in this book. The symbols ⊓ and ∨ in the strum patterns refer to down and up strokes, respectively. The letters in the pick patterns indicate which right-hand fingers play which strings.

p = thumb
i = index finger
m = middle finger
a = ring finger

For example: Pick Pattern 2 is played: thumb - index - middle - ring.

Strum Patterns

Pick Patterns

You can use the 3/4 Strum and Pick Patterns in songs written in compound meter (6/8, 9/8, 12/8, etc.). For example, you can accompany a song in 6/8 by playing the 3/4 pattern twice in each measure. The 4/4 Strum and Pick Patterns can be used for songs written in cut time (¢) by doubling the note time values in the patterns. Each pattern would therefore last two measures in cut time.